PAUL SHORE

UNCORKED

MY YEAR IN PROVENCE STUDYING PÉTANQUE, DISCOVERING CHAGALL, DRINKING PASTIS, AND MANGLING FRENCH

SEA TO SKY
BOOKS

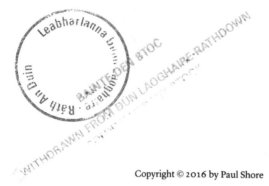

Sea to Sky Books
Whistler, BC

Cataloguing data available from Library and Archives Canada
ISBN 978-0-9813474-1-7 (paperback)
ISBN 978-0-9813474-2-4 (ebook)

Produced by Page Two
www.pagetwostrategies.com
Cover and interior design by Peter Cocking
Cover photo illustration: images courtesy iStock

17 18 19 20 21   5 4 3 2 1

CONTENTS

With love and thanks to Talya, Jashia, Aaron, Zelda,
Steve, and Hubert for their support and encouragement.

———————————————

And thank you to Jesse and Scott for
their guidance and patience.

A LITTLE BACKGROUND

Y OU MIGHT think this book is about wine, but it's not. It's about "uncorking" so much more in the culture of Provence and the Côte d'Azur, and the warmth that comes from learning to "smell the roses" and gradually being accepted in a foreign land.

I have tried to recreate events, locales, and conversations from memory, though my memory of these times has definitely faded and I often had to embellish. To maintain their anonymity, I have changed the names of some individuals, and substantially modified some people's characteristics. Any fun I poke at the French or their culture is done with a profound respect and care for them and the fierce way in which they protect their traditions. As I wrote, I tried to live by something Marc Chagall once said: "If I create from the heart, nearly everything works; if from the head, almost nothing."

PROLOGUE
WATCHING SILENTLY

COUNTED FOUR weathered old men, two of them holding shiny silver balls that filled both their hands, the other
two men grasping just one of those spheres in one hand.
Scattered around a tiny, bright yellow ball lying on the sandy
ground in front of the café were six more metal balls just like
those in the leathery hands. Those hands surely were cold,
since the January sun had just set behind the hills surrounding Saint-Paul de Vence, leaving the sky painted in soft pastel
colours all the way down to where it met the glimmering
surface of the Mediterranean Sea in the distance. I inhaled
deeply, the smoke from the men's cigarettes mixing with
the sweet smell of burning vineyard clippings to produce a
remarkably unique and pleasant scent.

Whatever this game was that they were so focused on, they were playing it in peace. They had the grounds to themselves at this quiet time of year, when the tourist hordes were back at home earning a living and the locals retired early each evening because of the short days and the chill in the air. The only interruptions came from passing mopeds that sputtered their way up the village's narrow cobblestone ring road every now and then, earning the riders looks of disdain from the players, who forced sharp exhales of smoke in unison from between pursed lips.

The only other people in sight were a couple seated in wicker chairs at a round, marble-topped table on the terrace of the café—he smoking, drinking an espresso, and listening; she talking passionately, yet softly enough not to distract the players or draw attention to herself. And there was also the surly barman serving three local gentlemen a liquor that turned cloudy white each time he topped up their glasses with water from a carafe—*pastis*. Plus me, perched on the stout, ancient, stone wall that surrounded the playing area and the few massive trees growing out of it, watching this mysterious game intently and silently, not daring to ask a single question of anybody.

I would learn soon that the game was called puh-taunq... *pétanque*. And that the great painter Marc Chagall had frequented this café with friends, while living in Saint-Paul. How was I going to gain entry into the arcane world of this ancient game with its half-understood rituals and ancient codes, and moreover, how was I going to embed myself deeply enough in Saint-Paul to understand even a little about its culture and history? I had no idea, though I was determined to do precisely that. But for the moment I was simply going to absorb the theatrics playing out in front of me, as the four crusty old men played, laughed, smoked, and, from time to time, kicked an unattended dog that wandered through their match.

1

A MYSTERIOUS GAME

T HE FRENCH word *bisou* is used to describe the charming manner in which the French greet one another with a ceremonial kiss on both cheeks. This act should not to be mistaken for a sign of real affection or even friendship, but rather as a refreshingly warm way of saying hello or goodbye.

As tourists in France, we foreigners have all been witness to these tiny gifts, though seldom do we gain admittance into the tightknit club of the 60 million or so people who exchange them. There are exceptions to the rule that a *bisou* does not convey real affection—one is the rare occasion when men exchange the pleasantry, rather than the typical handshake they nearly always use instead.

Receiving and delivering countless bisous during my year in the magical Côte d'Azur village of Saint-Paul de Vence made me feel a sense of "limited belonging," but when my neighbour, friend, and, most importantly, *pétanque* coach, Hubert, bid me farewell by initiating a bisou, after my last match and last pastis as a local, it gave me pause to reflect on how close I had become to this part of the world, its people, its culture, and the game I fell in love with the minute I first laid eyes on it: pétanque! And that ultimate bisou also made me realize just how much chutzpah it had taken to break into French culture by daring to play pétanque, never mind to succeed in becoming good at it.

For the uninitiated—in other words, anybody who isn't French (and, according to most of the people of France, that means Canada's Quebecois too)—pétanque looks a little like the Italian game of *bocce*, or the British game of lawn bowling, or even the winter sport of curling that is popular in Canada. Though I advise not to suggest such similarities out loud while standing on French soil, unless you have no desire to try to play the game, no desire to be welcomed into a café, no desire to gain the friendship of a local, and you desire to have the nickname Monsieur Con—the polite translation of which is, "village idiot." You see, pétanque IS uniquely French. It would be less of a faux-pas to say "Hey Jacques, this Châteauneuf-du-Pape is decent red wine, but it's a far cry from a Napa Valley red," than to say pétanque is similar to ANY other game.

To provide a thorough outline of the rules, strategy, and art—yes, art—of the game would require an anthology so detailed and so tedious to read, not to mention so difficult to obtain agreement on from even just a minyan[1] of French citizens, that I don't dare start down that path. Instead I offer up the following *précis*.

Pétanque is typically played between two teams of two players. The players tend to be middle-aged to elderly men, whose exposure to the sun from playing the game gives them a healthy, light-brown tinge, usually coupled with a skin texture similar to that of a well-aged French plum... i.e. a prune. These gentlemen speak seldom, and when they do open their mouths what is heard is usually slang or profanity, or silence followed by a *puff* of smoke from the drag they took of a cigarette several minutes earlier.

Having described the combatants, I'll move on to the playing surface, *le terrain,* and the equipment. For the purists pétanque isn't played on an organized field but on a small, open patch of grassless ground next to a public gathering place, like a café or a church. The grounds may be anything but uniform in size, shape, and consistency of dirt, and may include any number of obstacles, such as massive plane trees, café terraces, and elderly dogs. This non-uniformity is a big part of the charm and challenge of the game. Each player owns his or her personal set of three metal balls—or borrows a set from the nearby café, thereby indicating a lack of dedication to the game. To proudly and comfortably carry the heavy little metallic projectiles through the streets of one's beautiful 15th-century village on the way to a match, each ball owner also owns what can be best described as

---

1   In Judaism, a minyan is the quorum of ten Jewish adults required for certain religious obligations.

a mini leather briefcase precisely the size of three stacked balls. Tucked into corners of this little briefcase are two more crucial objects—first, a tiny towel for wiping dust from the balls and hands, to avoid the calamity of a ball slipping from one's hand during a play; and second, a tiny, coloured, wooden ball about the size of a plump cherry, which is the focal point of every throw. This small ball is the target that competitors attempt to park their metal balls closest to. This little round guy goes by many names: *bouchon* [cork], *cochonnet* [piglet], or simply *le petit*.

Which brings me to my favourite French word, *bouchon*—cork. The word gets used in my three favourite French pastimes: wine drinking, driving, and pétanque. Its use in driving is the least obvious, though every time I drove in Paris I saw it used in electronic signage that was flashing a message that read something like "*circulation bouchon* [traffic corked]." The word sounds so French and beautiful: *bouchon, bouchon, bouchon*. I just love saying it out loud.

But back to the game. The basic aim is to get at least one of your team's six balls closer to the bouchon than all of the other team's balls. Once all of the players have thrown or rolled all of their balls, if you're closest, you score one point, plus an additional point for each next closest ball that also belongs to your team—still with me? Now, scoring one single point is often a bad thing because it means you have to go first the next time the bouchon is tossed, which puts you at a disadvantage in that round... still with me? Oh, I forgot to mention that a match is made up of an indeterminate number of rounds, or "*mènes*"—or as we Canadians would call them in the icy game of curling, "ends," though in

that sport there is a minimum number of 10 ends, a rule that would be far too constraining for the magical game of pétanque. Each round starts with the tossing of the little bouchon ball, which becomes the target for the larger metal point-scoring balls. And each match culminates when one team reaches 13 total points and is leading by at least 2 points, after any number of rounds—still with me? Surely not.

Now the way you toss your metal ball can either take the form of rolling it, which is called "pointing" and which gets you dubbed the *pointeur* of your team, or throwing the ball in the air, which is called "shooting" and which earns you the name *tireur*.

Ok, I'll dispense with the rest of the basic, rudimentary, beginner's outline, now that you are gaining an appreciation for the complexity of the game and are surely beginning to see that if you mix in the requirements of sharp hand-eye coordination, strategy, and the art of playing psychological mind games, you really have something that is difficult to master. It's a bit like chess, if chess required coordination and keeping your eyes peeled so that a metal projectile didn't crush your toes. Note that I required several private tutor sessions simply to gain this rough level of understanding, so that I could watch others play and have a clue why they seem to be randomly tossing balls around a patch of dirt, showing a modest amount of care not to injure one another.

And so I turn back to how I came to arrive in Saint-Paul de Vence and my first encounter with this mysterious game. I had been to the Côte d'Azur as a Euro-Railing new university graduate a decade earlier. I'd scratched the surface of Nice, Cannes, and Monaco, like most narrow-minded, wide-eyed young travelers who do the typical 12-country, 37-city European "been there, done that, got the t-shirt" tour. All I recall from the Mediterranean portion of that trip is trying to catch glimpses of movie stars attending the famous Cannes Film Festival; eating excellent thin crust pizza in the *Vieille Ville* [Old Town] area of Nice; and gawking at the beauty of Monaco's apartments, yachts, sports cars, vistas, and women (especially the topless ones on the white smooth pebbly beach that felt like it was manicured daily). I was more impressed with cities like Paris, Florence, and Munich at that age.

In '96, I returned on a hurried business trip while working for a small software company. That trip had me looking at the South of France more deeply and appreciating its curious and mysterious culture. During the taxi ride that took me from the Nice airport to my first meeting with our business partner, Texas Instruments, the driver spoke to me in French and I said, *"je suis Canadien, mais mon français est très mal* [I am Canadian, but my French is very bad]." Without taking his hands off the wheel or his eyes off the road ahead, he replied by correcting my French: "*Mauvais* [bad]!" Hilarious, and without even so much as a smirk. I loved it. And so began my official addiction to the Côte d'Azur.

The very next evening of that same business trip, I had another humbling experience that further triggered my desire to learn about this culture. A colleague took me to dinner and instead of admitting that I couldn't make head or tail of the menu, I confidently ordered *soupe aux fruits de mer et poisson,* which I thought was soup, fruit, and fish in three separate courses. My French knowledge was too poor to understand that *fruits de mer*, which literally translates to "fruits of the sea," means *shellfish*. What I was served was an extremely aromatic (i.e. stinky) bowl of cold soup made from a variety shellfish and some kind of local whitefish—and at this point in my life I hardly cared for seafood of any kind, much less fish, crab, mussels, and prawn bits all together in a creamy cold soup. But I had to pretend that it was exactly what I was hoping for and choke back each spoonful of a concoction that must have been a delight to the palates of most locals.

As my flight back to Canada gently climbed out of Nice on a gorgeous summer evening, I finally managed to focus on the beauty of the region. I looked down to the blue-green waters of the Mediterranean with its rocky cliffs and beaches, the yachts dotting the water, the city and the little perched villages in the surrounding hills, and beyond the foothills of the snow-covered Alps. I fell into a trance, mesmerized by the image below me that appeared more like an impressionist's work of art than a real place. Once we passed the Alps, I snapped back to the reality of my high-tech life in a start-up software company and thought to myself, "Hell, if we ever open an office in Europe and choose to locate it here, they can count me in for that job." Remarkably, within a year I learned that dreaming big can pay off, as an outpost in the Nice area became a reality, with me as its sole initial employee—French Riviera, here I come!

My employer hired a firm that would help me find a place to live. I told them that I wanted to live in a "cute small town, away from the busy coast" and, after viewing some terrible little apartments, I jumped at the opportunity to rent a cool, cave-like apartment in a tiny town I'd never heard of named Saint-Paul de Vence. Little did I realize that I was about to take up residence in a village that could be best described in summer as "gaudy tourist central" because it was so famous and magical that it drew visitors from around the world. Nor did I know that the brilliant modernist painter Marc Chagall had lived, worked, and was buried in my soon-to-be-surrogate hometown. Nor did I have a clue that Saint-Paul was tantamount to a holy site for an odd game called pétanque. Yes, I was pretty much completely ignorant of the remarkable history of Saint-Paul and the special place it held in the heart of French art and culture. At times, I would feel like the stereotypical American tourist that I would come to hear my neighbours complain about, as they told exaggerated stories like the one in which a tourist says, "France is great, but the food is lousy and it is impossible to get a good cheeseburger here."

2

PICTURE POSTCARD

_____

SAINT-PAUL IS a picture-postcard village. As you climb the windy road inland from the *autoroute* that connects Nice and Cannes, you pass quaint old towns, farms, and vineyards, now and then catching brief, teasing, peekaboo views of Saint-Paul perched on a hill up ahead. Only as you navigate the last veer in the road before the town does the full beauty of the village and its medieval walls and clock tower show itself fully, along with its backdrop of the Maritime Alps. The colours and scents of the flowers of the region seem to intensify as the road climbs, culminating in a floral explosion of purples, yellows, oranges, and reds as you reach the stony entrance of Saint-Paul. And just before the village entrance is a turn off to a remarkable place that often goes unnoticed at first, due to its odd, non-descriptive name—a museum of modern art named Foundation Maeght.

Aimé and Marguerite Maeght's house had been next to Marc Chagall's, and the museum has several of his works in its permanent collection, including Les Amoureux, a large mosaic that welcomes visitors at the entrance, and La Vie, an immense painting whose colours jump out of the canvas. Encouraged by their artist friends, the Maeghts founded the art foundation after the tragic death of their young son in 1953, and for over fifty years now it has contributed to Saint-Paul de Vence's reputation for culture. Several artists, including Giacometti, Miro, and Braque, assisted with the garden, which features sculptures, a pond with an inlaid mosaic bottom, and a maze. What great fortune that I had so unwittingly stumbled into living in a place that would soon open my eyes to French culture and art in general.

After taking over the keys to my new medieval apartment, complete with medieval headroom that ensures that only a field mouse does not have to duck through every doorway, I went for a stroll to check out my new surroundings, and my sure-to-be-welcoming co-villagers. Within the roughly 300 metres by 100 metres inside of Saint-Paul's walls, plus the area just outside of its walls, live maybe 500 residents. The focal point of the village is Le Café de la Place and the rough piece of ground in front of it, which appeared off limits to anyone except older men (and the occasional brave woman) tossing what seemed to be small cannon balls. Being the type who considers any game that involves any kind of ball, in any form of motion, to be all the evidence required to prove

that human beings have indeed evolved into the most highly intelligent life form in the universe, I quickly gravitated to "the ball playing place" by the main café.

It was as if an invisible force pulled me there and instructed me to watch, learn and play. Every week I would sit for hours watching, but unable to learn much due to my lack of French language skills and the fact that small-statured Canadians appeared to be completely invisible to Frenchmen playing games. It was like this was only a dream and I didn't really exist in France, sitting on a little wall with my feet dangling into the playing area, as the combatants were oblivious to my presence. Fortunately, I didn't have to pinch my own arm to prove to myself that I was really there because, the minute an incoming ball rolled anywhere near my feet, the yelps of the grumpy old men proved that I was, in fact, quite visible. For an instant I thought, "How kind; they care for my safety," but as soon as I looked into their eyes I realized what their yells really must have meant something like, "Move your damn foot you idiot tourist, before it disrupts our game."

Nonetheless, I was beginning to "interact" with the locals, if only in a superficial manner. Now I'm a university-educated engineer who prides himself on being able to figure out complex, puzzling problems, and yet no matter how long I watched and attempted to dissect this game, its rules remained a mystery to me. I was quickly gaining an immense new respect for the French, who had somehow managed to encrypt the real essence of this game hundreds of years ago, so that no foreigner could take it back to his or her own country simply by observing it. Again, I love any game involving rolling motions (i.e. involving balls, discs, pucks, etc.) and I was determined to become a pétanque player, but I was at a loss for how to even begin to break into this tight little fraternity that seemed to require at least two qualities that were going to be very hard to fake ... being over 40 and being French.

3

YOU NEED A SPONSOR

U NFORTUNATELY, LEISURE time was at a premium for me, since unlike the local Saint-Paul *pétanquers*, I had rather inadvertently pursued a career in what I now understand to be a world of self-sacrifice for work and money at the expense of just about everything else. My dedication to my work had me flying off most weeks to different glamorous European cities, which I hardly got to see. But since I had to drive directly past the pétanque grounds each time I returned to the village, the mysterious game never left my mind for very long.

My moving into Saint-Paul was similar to a new animal being introduced into a small zoo. The existing inhabitants intently watched my every move—when I awoke and left my cave each day; when I returned; where I ate and drank; and which other animals I socialized with. The curious looks on the faces of my neighbours and the local shopkeepers, as I greeted them with a simple "Bonjour!" each time I departed to and returned from the Nice airport, told me that they all thought, "What is this odd little Canadian, who speaks French badly and drags a heavy suitcase up and down our cobblestone streets, doing here? What illicit business is he running from our town? He seems friendly, but surely he can't be trusted." I could picture them holed up in a café debating the possibilities in whispers, as they *puffed* on cigarettes and drank espresso. Of course, rarely did anybody ever ask me what I did for a living. It was as if they preferred not to know, so as not to incriminate themselves, or maybe not knowing enabled continuous new gossip during quiet times when the throngs of loud, over-bearing, uncultured tourists took breaks to escape the summer heat. What did eventually become clear to me, though only after living for a year in their town and then returning home to work for many years more in the technology industry, was that their knowing glances had been trying to communicate to me to slow down, smell the roses and the coffee (literally in this town), and be sure that I was enjoying both my work hours and my leisure time—or as Marc Chagall once said, "Work isn't to make money; you work to justify life."

Between business road trips I had committed myself to the excruciating task of improving my 11th-grade-dropout French skills, by signing up with a private tutor. Colette was a delightful, older lady who had been tutoring expats like me for thirty years. After only a few lessons, I came to regard her as equal parts French teacher, cultural coach, and shrink, as she guided me through what to her must have been the predictable trials and tribulations of someone learning a new language and culture in a foreign land. She was a very *petite* older woman who exuded class out of every pore and who spoke English as impeccable as her French. Her wisdom was frequently clear, which she highlighted early on by mentioning that expats typically become comfortable with the language and somewhat comfortable with the culture after about one year, which sadly is also typically when they return home—how prophetic that would turn out to be for me.

One day I worked up the nerve to ask Colette a question that I knew wouldn't have a simple answer. I couldn't do so using my brutal French, even though she actually encouraged me to brutalize her language so that I could learn more quickly from my mistakes—some classes seemed like nothing but mistake-correction exercises. In fact, Colette often pointed out to me that many words are close cousins of English words, and encouraged me to simply say the English word with a French accent if I sensed that the French word might be similar. But in this case the topic was too important and I wanted to be sure that we communicated clearly, so I asked the question in English: "What is this game I regularly watch by the café, while doing the homework you give me, that is played by older men using metal balls?"—maybe I should have just asked in French.

Colette chuckled and shook her head from side to side as she sighed, then answered, "Pétanque."

Ah ha! Now I had the official name; this was progress. I asked why she was shaking her head in a negative way and yet smirking at the same time. She told me it was a very old

French game, played only by Frenchmen. When I replied that "Soon it would also be played by a little Canadian," her smirk changed to real laughter. I said, "Come on, why not?"

Colette replied by cautioning me that attempting to break into this fraternity likely would not be a pleasant experience, but if I insisted on trying it I must find a "sponsor."

"A sponsor?" I asked, thinking that I hadn't seen "Coca-Cola" or "Michelin" or even "Ricard's Pastis" on the back of the players' shirts.

"Yes, a sponsor or a coach, if you prefer to call him that. You can't just waltz onto the grounds and invite yourself to play—you'll be laughed away from the café forever and maybe even laughed out of the village—you might have to relocate, maybe even flee the country."

OK, now I knew she was exaggerating, but I got the point. I needed a private tutor for this aspect of French life too.

Wow, what a dilemma. I hardly knew a soul at any level deeper than "Bonjour," except for Hubert (pronounced 'hue-bear'), my quirky neighbour who ran the only high-tech outfit in Saint-Paul and had therefore taken some interest in me because I was also a techie. Hubert spoke perfect English and didn't like speaking French with me because he couldn't stand listening to me trash his language and he didn't have the patience to correct my errors. As a result, he was a Frenchman that I already communicated well with because he always forced the conversation into my language.

Hubert was vertically challenged, like me; his eyes were deep-set and scrutinizing; and his hair dark and thinning. I had an immediate affinity for him because of his vibrant character, determined conduct, dramatic flare, cleverness of a fox, and bold and blameless manner. An exchange between us several months later, after he resurrected a dead cell phone of mine that I had dropped in the salt water of the Mediterranean, epitomizes the man and the playful relationship we developed.

He came to me gloating that he had fixed the phone, which I had given up for dead, by using a *lave-vaiselle* [dishwasher]. He was proud that it worked perfectly now, except the microphone was still a bit intermittent. He boasted that he had simply opened it and placed both halves in the dishwasher to blast the dried salt from the sea out of it, and *voila,* it worked again. I laughed and told him, "With technical skills like that, you should go work for that fine German aerospace company, Airbus," which, of course, I knew would get under his skin because the company is a pan-European partnership with its headquarters in France. He fired back with, "You should go home to Canada now, and spend some time in Québec, where the best skiing and only real culture are."

I probably wouldn't have dared to ask Hubert about pétanque had I not felt that I had already accidentally endeared myself to him a few days before. You see, my funky cave-like apartment looked directly down onto the ring road that runs within the ancient walls of the town, and each night a tiny garbage truck would make its rounds on this road. The miniature truck looked custom made for Saint-Paul's one road and many pedestrian pathways—it was an engineering marvel, except that it made just as much noise as its full-scale relatives. It made a pick-up of cans directly below my bedroom window at 2 am and was oddly on time every single night, except for weekends when I didn't need to be as well rested the next morning.

After the first couple weeks of this surprise "feature" of my apartment, which might have explained why the rent was only extremely high, rather than ridiculously high, I was ready to snap from sleep deprivation and went to consult my one friend in town, Hubert. I launched into somewhat of a rant, "What's with that *camion de poubelle* [garbage can truck] that comes past at 2:00 every night? . . . it breaks up my REM sleep and I'm falling apart . . . *regarde mes valises* [look at my bags]!," as I pointed to the area below both my eyes. I have to do something about this and get its schedule changed."

Hubert burst into all-out gut-wrenching laughter, repeating my rather nonsensical phrase camion de poubelle several times in the middle of his laughter. When he'd caught his breath he said, "*Bonne chance* [good luck] the *marie* [city hall] is in charge of garbage collection and there is no way you will get that bureaucracy to change anything for you, Mr. Canadian."

In disgust I walked away, saying "We'll see about that" and heading straight to the beautiful old city hall building in the center of the village. When I arrived and introduced myself to the administrator at the front desk in French, making use of the greeting "*enchanté* [enchanted to meet you]" in an attempt to be charming, I immediately launched into the same camion de poubelle rant I had delivered to Hubert, though this time I was a little less emphatic and much more pleading in nature and spoke only in my broken French, rather than mixing two languages. As I concluded my plea with "Regarde mes valises" and a very distraught look on my face, the poor woman seemed stunned. It took a few minutes

before she said that she would look into the matter—I think that I had inadvertently scared her a little and she simply wanted to be sure that I left the building without incident.

Miraculously, that very night the garbage truck stopped passing my place in the middle of the night, so I went to see Hubert first thing in the morning to brag about my victory. It was clear that he was impressed, though he didn't want to admit it, and hastened to add, "You know this means that the truck is now waking somebody else in the middle of the night—who is probably a long-time local."

"*C'est la vie* [that's life]; it's not waking me up anymore," I replied. It was at that moment that I think it struck Hubert that I just might have a few ounces of French blood in me and therefore we could be real friends—I even overheard him tell that story, in French, to several friends of his, which was a clear sign that he loved that I had had the nerve to attempt what I did.

So with Colette's talk of a "sponsor" weighing heavily on my mind, the next time I saw Hubert I asked what I knew to be a stupid, yet necessary, question: "Hubert, do you play pétanque?" This is when I got my formal introduction to that somewhat rude French gesture I refer to as *la puff*. It involves taking a slow deep inhale on a cigarette, rolling the eyes back in the head, and then exhaling the smoke (either rapidly or slowly) in the general direction of the question asker. The best I have been able to interpret this gesture to means is, "The question you just asked is so stupid that the only response it deserves is an exhale of smoke in your face!"

After I had dodged the smoke cloud and still looked puzzled, Hubert finally said, "Of course I play pétanque; I'm French."

I took a step back to put a little more distance between us, readied myself for another *la puff* of smoke and dared to utter my brilliant follow-up question: "Will you teach me to play?" This was quickly met by the only *grande puff* I experienced the entire year I lived in France.

Offended to have been dismissed so easily I said, "Why not? I know I can be good at it!"

Hubert simply countered with the tough-to-debate, "YOU ARE NOT FRRRREENCH!!"

Not one to take *Non*, or any form of smoke exhalation, as an answer, I countered with "OK, then I'll find somebody else to teach me because I AM going to learn to play this game." And with that, I stormed off into my cave apartment, slamming my replica 15th-century heavy wooden door for effect.

After I cooled off and emerged from my self-imposed dungeon, I immediately ran into Hubert again. As I attempted to avoid him, he said, "*Attends* [Wait]," which in itself seemed odd to me.

What followed was a complete shock. Hubert whispered, "OK, I'll teach you."

"What was that?" I replied, "I don't think I heard you correctly."

To which he said, "Shut up before I change my mind; you heard me." Actually he said "*Ferme ta gueule* [Shut your beak]" not "Shut up."

When I impulsively blurted out, "Great, let's go," Hubert replied, still whispering as if the local Culture Police might be listening, "No, not now, you fool; I'll come find you when it's time."

4

A CLANDESTINE AFFAIR

OVER THE next few days I anxiously awaited a signal from Hubert that my first lesson in pétanque would begin. Each time I would see him, I would think to myself, "This is the day; this is the time," but he would talk about other things and not even mention the potential for playing a game soon. I began to wonder if he had forgotten about his loose promise, maybe purposely.

Then one summer evening as I returned home very late from work, Hubert startled me in the darkness of our shared alley—it was like he had been lying in wait to attack some prey—as he threw open his office door and whispered, "*Maintenant* [Now]."

I replied, "Maintenant what?" and he said in a very mat-ter-of-fact way, "I teach you pétanque now."

It occurred to me that I had rarely seen people play pétanque at night, though there were lights hanging from the beautiful old trees that surrounded Saint-Paul's playing grounds. It just seemed completely unnecessary—surely 18 hours of sunlight was enough to get one's daily fill of pétan-que? So this is how it had to be, a clandestine affair—Hubert was too ashamed, or nervous, or proud to teach a Canadian this ancient French game in the light of day. Whatever, it didn't matter to me; I was thrilled that I was going to start learning. Even if I was made to feel like some kind of inde-cent criminal while learning; even if I would have to play for the rest of my life under the cloak of darkness; and even if I would have to sign in blood that I would never disclose pub-licly that I had been taught to understand a piece of ancient French culture—I was about to play pétanque!

I quickly ran into my apartment, threw my briefcase inside, changed into some comfortable clothes, grabbed a hunk of cheese and a stale baguette to serve as my dinner, and ran back outside to find Hubert before he changed his mind. As we walked together down the dark cobblestone streets towards the famous grounds, which I was finally going to be permitted to set foot on, hardly a word was spo-ken. It felt as if Hubert was concerned that somebody might spot us from an upper-story window and call the authorities because it was suspicious behaviour to be walking so late at night with a known foreign infiltrator.

When we arrived at the café it dawned on me that Hubert had his own set of pétanque balls in his personal carrying case, yet I had none. He walked me into the still open café, curtly introduced me to the bartender and asked in French for a loaner set of balls. There was an uncomfortable pause for a few seconds as the barman's eyes surveyed me. He thought things over for what seemed like an eternity, then nodded gently and reached below the counter to retrieve a heavy little package that he handed to me in a half-hearted, very cautious manner. I accepted the package carefully, like it was a fragile set of crystal wine glasses, nodded back and softly said "*Merci*," then turned to follow Hubert outside. Other than a few semi-inebriated patrons on the café terrace engaged in serious conversations about the past day's crop of obnoxious foreign tourists, their issues with their mistresses, and the general malaise of the state of France, there was nobody around to witness what was about to transpire—treason.

I was itching to get going with my first lesson. But not so fast little, sporty, hockey-playing Canadian; first there were other introductory topics to be covered. Like unpacking the little purse-like bag and reviewing its contents: three heavy metal balls about the size of baseballs (sorry to all Frenchmen/women for making this comparison); one brightly coloured (usually yellow or green) *cochonnet* (or *bouchon* or *le petit*), a little smaller than a ping-pong ball and somewhere between the weight of a ping-pong ball and a golf ball, which would become the target in the match; and one small cloth similar to the cloth you use to clean your eyeglasses, for wiping dust off of one's balls or off of one's hands.

Then there was a pause to touch on a little history to help instill in me the significance of being allowed to walk on the hallowed, dusty ground, on which we now stood. Hubert said in a very serious and somewhat somber tone, "Do you realize that Yves Montand played on this ground?"

I answered this hallowed revelation with a mistake so grave it nearly cost me my chance to play; I said, "Who is she, Yves Montagne?" Three mistakes in just five words! 1) Yves is a male French name, not female. 2) It is "Montand," not "Montagne," one of the rare nouns that I recognize easily, meaning "mountain"; 3) He was a famous, highly regarded, very good-looking French actor and singer whose career spanned from the 1940s through the 1980s.

Hubert paused, his eyes bulged out slightly, he gave me one of those characteristically French *puffs* (smoke included), and said with disdain, "You don't know Yves MONTAND, the famous actor who bedded Marilyn Monroe?" The only thing worse I could have done, than not knowing of him, would have been to point out that he was Italian born, a true fact, but not one that would have been appreciated. Fortunately, since I was completely oblivious to Yves and only read up on him later, I did not make that mistake.

In response to Hubert's question and his *puff,* I gave a good French shoulder shrug and said, "Nope, *je suis désolé* [I'm sorry], though I can understand now just how important this Saint-Paul ground of pétanque is." I then held my breath and hoped this response had been both flippant and respectful enough that we could continue without an evening-long lesson on 20th-century French cinema and song. Hubert smirked, shook his head slowly side to side to indicate my pathetic sheltered Canadian existence, and turned to walk out onto the dark, dusty, partly lit ground. I followed.

"OK, we need to determine if you are a *pointeur* or a *tireur*," he said.

"First, could you explain to me what the difference is?" I replied.

Another *puff* of smoke wafted across my face and into my lungs. Hubert explained that a *pointeur* is the teammate who goes first and who most likely will be called on throughout the match to use finesse to slowly roll balls with great aiming ability and understanding for how the ground will affect the path of the slowly rolling ball, his goal being to gently park his balls closest to the *bouchon*. He went on to explain that the *tireur* is the teammate most likely to be called on to throw balls in the air all the way from his hand to the mélange of balls near the bouchon, in an attempt to strike or "shoot" opponents balls and surgically remove them from their advantageous positions.

With this new knowledge, I said with over-confidence, "Oh, I'll be good at both of those."

Another *puff* of smoke wafted across my face and into my lungs, after which Hubert said, "I prefer to be the tireur, so you are the pointeur." So it seemed that the role I would play had been decided without me so much as demonstrating coordination once.

Having dispensed with the tireur-pointeur decision, Hubert pulled his *bouchon* from his pocket and tossed it in what appeared to be a random direction and distance, then dragged one heel across the ground to scratch a line that we would throw all our balls from during this round. He then explained that the *bouchon* has to travel between six and ten strides (metres, technically, though strides will suffice for measurement purposes, rather than resorting to something so exact and inartistic as a tape-measure) before it comes to rest. The little target ball was also not allowed to stop within a couple of feet of any perceived obstacle for the toss to be considered a valid toss and therefore one that we could then use as the starting point for a round.

Now "perceived" obstacle turns out to be in the eye of the beholder—some consider a tree to be an obstacle, some not; a tourist is definitely not an obstacle because they could easily be intimidated into moving simply by uttering any curt French expression forcefully in their general direction; a sleeping dog is generally accepted to be an obstacle; and dog poop is very certainly an obstacle.

Hubert's first toss of the *cochonnet* was of course satisfactory. And since we had no other team to play, not that Hubert would have considered being my teammate just yet, we began to play one-on-one against each other. He went first to demonstrate how to throw, which is a distinct disadvantage because whoever goes second can attempt to remove or go around the other's ball. He threw underhand and the ball only travelled in the air a few feet and then its impact kicked up a mini dust cloud, before it rolled to within about two feet of the little target ball.

Now it was my first turn, so I stepped up and tossed the ball overhand like a baseball pitch—it skidded past the target at high speed and nearly disappeared out of sight. More *puff*-ing sounds and smoke filled the air—"*Mer-de*" I heard.

"What's that you said about 'the sea', 'la mer'?" I said.

To which he snapped back, "I didn't say anything about the damn sea . . . I said, 'Shit', what are you doing?"

I told him I was applying my own style, to which he replied, "If you want to only play with me once, and to lose to tourists forever, keep that up; otherwise start trying to copy my proper form." I felt like Tim Robbins' charter in the 1988 baseball movie, Bull Durham, who was given the demeaning nickname 'Meat' by Kevin Costner's character—listen to the experienced guru veteran, you meathead, or have him purposefully set you up to go down in flames. With that I changed my attitude and did my best to mimic Hubert's every move.

It turned out this was going to be far harder to get good at than I had ever expected. It was like learning to bowl on a rough, inconsistent, dirt surface, on which the target is one tiny "pin," rather than ten large pins. Oh, and that tiny pin can be moved any time by being contacted by other balls, all while your opponents are hurling subtle verbal abuse at you in a language that isn't your mother tongue. Hubert didn't offer much more coaching during the rest of our first match, clearly to teach me a lesson about not listening and about some hard realities of the world. It was much like a parent allowing a toddler to fall flat on his face a few times to learn about the inescapable force of gravity, while the falls are still minor enough not to result in permanent injury or mental scarring. The result was a quickly executed drubbing—where I come from we would refer to it as being "skunked" or "shut out" or "blanked" or simply "humiliated." The first player to reach 13 points, tallied over however many rounds are required to reach 13, is the winner—and he won 13-0!

There wasn't much I could have done to avoid this, but had I known of the tradition that Hubert introduced me to right after the slaughter was complete, I certainly would have focused harder on trying to score at least one measly point towards the end of the debacle. After his last throw had confirmed the completion of the trouncing, Hubert quietly picked up his balls, walked over to me, shook my hand, said "*Bon match*," and then sat down at the café and ordered two glasses of pastis, which I learned later would be mine to pay for. Then he stood up and said, "Follow me; I need to show you something on the wall at the end of the bar."

I had no idea what I would be shown something in a bar, that I hadn't already seen in a bar somewhere in the world. I followed with my tail between my legs and my head hanging low. As we neared the far end of the room, I noticed what appeared to be a picture frame shrouded by a small set of curtains with a bell mounted beside it on the wall. Was I about to have to watch a puppet show as the penalty for losing my first match so soundly? No, I was about to have to pucker up and "kiss the Fanny."

I have since done some homework and discovered that the original Fanny was a sweet young lady who worked in a café near a pétanque court in the 1800s. Whenever a person or a team had been humiliated by scoring absolutely no points in a loss, Fanny's heart would go out to them. To ease their pain, she would allow the losers to kiss her on the cheek. Then one day when the mayor of her village, who she despised deeply, lost a pétanque match 13 to 0 and went to Fanny for the consolation kiss, she stepped up onto a chair, bent over and lifted her skirt, and said, "You can kiss this!" The surprised mayor obliged and planted a kiss on her derriere, and the next team that lost by a shut-out was asked to plant a kiss in the same place.

Fanny must have had quite the bum because this part of her anatomy soon became the location of choice for all defeated teams. The ceremony quickly spread throughout the pétanque world and female drink-servers all over the south of France carried on the tradition established by the first young Fanny. At some stage the eager losers faced a shortage of compassionate female servers willing to continue this practice, so pétanque clubs had to resort to posters or sculptures of Fanny. And that is what was behind the little set of curtains at our café: a bust (I really do mean a three-dimensional model) of a bare naked lady's bottom entitled "Fanny," ready for a kiss and a ringing of the bell to draw the attention of the entire bar, town, and possibly the surrounding countryside. In a rare display of what I viewed as a form of chivalry, Hubert treated my loss as only a "Fanny warning" and a part of my education. Since I had not been told in advance about the tradition, he did not ring the bell, nor did he make me kiss the sculpture of buttocks. Even more kindly, he didn't make me pay for the drinks of all the patrons remaining in the bar at that odd hour, though he did make me pay for his pastis, which I thought was very fair.

And so my clandestine initiation into the game—no, "the world"—of pétanque came to a close with a wide variety of lessons learned on a dark, humid, quiet summer night in Saint-Paul de Vence.

5

CULTURE SHOCK

NEVER REALLY had to remind myself that I had been sent to France for work, rather than to conduct a study for *National Geographic* on the different varietals of lavender or to learn a new pastime for my retirement years. It was the need for a regular paycheque that kept the reality of work-first-play-later front and center in my head. Adapting to work-life in my new setting had been challenging, especially during the first few weeks, which dealt me some setbacks that I would only look back on and laugh about years later.

I had set up shop in a shared office complex in the heart of France's mini Silicon Valley, a technology park between Nice and Cannes named Sophia Antipolis. Everything about working in Sophia was a challenging adventure in my early days there. My co-workers typically took lunch breaks from noon until close to 2 pm, and when I tried to use this time to run errands, I received a rude awakening to the slower pace of life that really took me by surprise. For example, banks and many other businesses closed from 12 to 2. This put a real dent in getting errands done over a sandwich on-the-go, though it of course made for some daily peaceful downtime, if one was inclined to allow oneself to relax in the middle of the workday.

Even buying a panini lunch from the food truck turned out to be more difficult than I expected the first time around. I confidently ordered a chicken panini and a soda: "*Je voudrais un panini de poulet et un Orangina.*" (By the way, Orangina is a very popular orange soda that comes in a glass bottle shaped like an orange—*magnifique!*) My confidence was quickly shattered when the cute food truck lady told me the price and what I heard was "*trente deux deux francs.*" I panicked, feeling my face heat up and turn red in an instant. "Thirty two two francs" is what I translated in my head as I replied, "*Je suis desolé, trente deux deux?* [Sorry, thirty two two?]" A kind foreigner behind me in line, who likely was envisioning his two-hour lunch break slipping away due to my ineptitude, saved the day by explaining to me that the woman was saying "*tren-te deux* [thirty-two]" in her southern France accent that often adds a syllable to words. Every day thereafter, when I ordered my favourite panini lunch, I would say, "*Ah oui, tren-TE deux* [Oh yes, thirty-two]," as I passed her my 32 francs with a flirty smile of accomplishment on my face.

When I finally did find a bank that was open for a few hours per day, I had another trying discussion, despite it being completely in English. This experience at the local Banc Nationale de Paris spread out over a week and two separate visits, and was almost like the famous Abbott and Costello "Who's On First" vaudeville routine, a circular, frustrating conversation. During the first visit the teller explained that to open a bank account I needed a home address and a phone number, but when I went to France Telecom they told me I couldn't have a phone without a bank account. And when I went to rent my apartment later that week I was told that I couldn't sign a lease without a bank account and a phone number. So back to the bank I went in a huff, wondering if this time they would add to the list of requirements "a nice haircut administered by a regional *coiffeur*, and the contact details of a contracted French language tutor." After requesting to speak to the manager, who immediately went to a back room and apparently convened a meeting more complex than the Versailles Peace Conference, I was told they would make a rare exception because they thought they could trust me. Wow, lucky for me, they would allow me to open a bank account and keep my money with them, without either a home address or a phone number, as long as I promised with a handshake to return with both by the end of the week—temper tantrum averted.

Next came the challenge of buying a simple Internet router box for use in my office. Now this was before the age of online shopping, and in hindsight I should have visited a local computer shop in person, but instead I dared to call a shop and order by phone. The guy on the phone tried to sell me a device from a European brand that I didn't recognize, but I insisted on a US product that I was confident in. After some grumbling, he agreed to order it for me. When the box arrived at my office, I gleefully opened it with an air about me of "See, I can do this; I can survive here." In an instant, that bubble was to burst in my face, as I saw that the power cord had come with two bare wires and no plug to enable it to be inserted into a wall outlet. Unbelievable!

I was incensed and picked up the phone to dial the guy's number, pounding on each key as I dialed. When I calmly explained the problem to him in French, he simply replied, "*C'est normal, monsieur.*" I lost control, switched to English and ranted, "No, it is not normal to deliver a piece of electronic equipment with bare wires and no way to plug it in … where am I to put the wires, in my ears?" The moment I uttered those words, I realized I had provided a very easy path to being told to put the wires in a different orifice, but somehow the rude fellow didn't choose to stoop that low and instead said in English, "You insisted on ordering that American product, despite my advice to the contrary, and when it ships to Europe they don't put a plug on the cord because they don't provide a warranty for use outside of the U.S., so they want you to have to install your own plug onto it, sir." My rant only grew more intense: "You knew that and didn't tell me that when I ordered? Do you think I have a lab and a soldering iron here, monsieur?" That brought to a close our conversation, as he calmly said, "*C'est normal monsieur, au revoir*" and with that the line went dead. I then did a fit-to-be-tied *C'est normal* dance of frustration in my office, which luckily nobody saw (though some nearby probably heard), and went out to locate a shop that could solder a connector onto my two bare wires, my head having been reprogrammed for a new definition of "customer service."

If cultural and language challenges were not enough, on my first formal visit to the head offices of our partner Texas Instruments on the outskirts of Nice, I learned that my Canadian-style French was not only *mauvais*. It was also rife with words I knew to be correct at home, yet that were incorrect in France. After temporarily parking just outside of the main doors and sauntering into the lobby with a put-on display of confidence, while boiling inside with nervous energy, I said to the receptionist, "*Bonjour mademoiselle, pouvez-vous me dire où est le stationnement pour les visiteurs* [Hello miss, can you tell me where the visitor parking is]?" I grew up in Ottawa, across the river from Québec, where it turns out the French language has in some ways evolved slower than in France. I had grown familiar with the Quebecois term for "parking spot," *stationnement*, because it is written on signs all over Ottawa. Yet the lovely young receptionist scrunched up her face and said in an extremely condescending manner with a strong French accent, "'le parking'?" Ah OK; just as my tutor had told me, here in France one can often get away with simply taking a modern English word and pronouncing it with a French accent ... mental note reinforced.

One of my first business meetings quickly brought me up to speed on the state of smoker/non-smoker relations in France. The engineering team I was visiting at France Telecom assisted each other in chain-smoking by silently offering one another cigarettes just as anybody's smoke was about to die out. It was like they were part of a brotherhood, who could sense each time a friend was about to risk taking a breath of fresh air and who always acted decisively to prevent that horror from ever happening. They exhaled directly into the center of the meeting; collectively managing to keep up a permanent thick cloud that made the difference between smoking and not smoking nil.

I travelled for business almost incessantly that year, including trips all over France and to Germany, Italy, Spain, Holland, England, Scandinavia, and Israel. Nearly every city in every country I visited was fascinating in one way or another, though each time I flew back into Nice I felt an odd calm fall over me, a calm associated with familiarity and belonging.

Each return flight tended to land in Nice by passing over the city once and then circling over the Mediterranean before commencing final approach. This always gave me a few minutes to look down at the fascinating region I was now calling home for some undetermined period of time and reflect on my good fortune. I often stared at the Promenade des Anglais from high above, reminiscing about evenings spent rollerblading on its boardwalk with my colleagues from Texas Instruments. The setting was gorgeous: the deep blue water of the Mediterranean to one side, the old city of Nice to the other, and my athletic, good-looking, young, international friends rollerblading in a little pack. The group was made up of mostly French men and women, plus a number of expats from all over the world. Some said that they loved my skating style because I looked like a hockey player, which gave me great joy, since I really was a terrible skater for a Canadian born in snowy Ottawa. The

simple act of skating fast for miles with these young friends on beautiful, hot, humid, summer evenings along the French Riviera, trading amusing stories and clever little insults in a mix of French and English, brought a calm sense of belonging washing over me.

And each time that I navigated the hustle and bustle of the airport, and then the rally-car style traffic on the way back to Saint-Paul, my calm would intensify as I reached the village entrance—if calmness is something that can intensify, though this sure seemed to be the case for me at these moments.

As I flashed my plastic local's card and exchanged nods of recognition with one of the security officers, who controlled vehicle entry to the inside of the ramparts, I would feel a sense of being home again. For a moment, I would gaze over my right shoulder to see who was playing pétanque in front of the café or sipping coffee on its terrace. After absorbing that scene for only a couple seconds, I would then turn my attention back forward to bob and weave around picture-taking tourists. These visitors were always oblivious to an oncoming car inside the village, until you dropped the clutch and revved the engine to send them scattering like rats at night caught in a spotlight—which makes me think that the upcoming proliferation of nearly-silent electric vehicles is going to make avoiding collisions with these folks much more difficult in the future! As I sped along, I would pass little restaurants and wave to the owners if they happened to be on a smoke break outside soaking in some sun, gradually making my way around the narrow ring-road just inside the stone walls of my ancient village. I would park in the well-hidden little gravel lot at the back of town, which had a secret exit through the steep forest behind town that led back down to the autoroute, and I would always grin as I began the stroll back to my apartment.

The short walk up the pedestrian, cobblestone, narrow alleys typically involved even more dodging of tourists, though on winter evenings the journey was beautifully quiet and void of people. On those evenings I could absorb the wide variety of pastel-painted doors and windows and ornate water fountains that lined my walk. In any season it was impossible not to notice the intense colours and scents of the massive flowering plants that climbed trellises and rocky apartment walls all the way home. And in the early winter months bright oranges and lemons adorned short little trees just beside the car park. I would see familiar faces and exchange simple friendly greetings without breaking stride, at times stopping in to chat with a gallery owner who had nobody to speak with at the time I happened to be passing by.

When I entered my little cave-like apartment, I would always go to the window that opened on to my one-foot-wide balcony and take in the view past the rampart walls of the Maritime Alps and the rocky hills before them, while breathing in the humid fragrant air. I had quickly become at ease in this place, far more easily than in any other foreign place I had ever spent time in.

6

INITIATION BY GENDARMES

FOR SEVERAL weeks my one-on-one instructional sessions with Hubert continued under the shroud of darkness. I never played so poorly again as to have him hold me to zero points, therefore preventing my friend the pleasure of seeing me buy a round of drinks for the bar and more importantly preventing me from being required to smooch the Fanny—funny how motivating humiliation-avoidance can be!

Under Hubert's often blunt and sarcastic tutelage, I slowly improved, gradually losing to him by less and less. More importantly, I was slowly impressing upon him that I was a decent strategist, a good listener when I wanted to be, and had sound hand-eye coordination as a base to build upon. There were two common themes that my coach often applied, as he taught me in his own unique and colourful way—a manner that became a large part of what I came to love about learning the game from Hubert. First, pétanque is like driving: "Stay down the middle of the highway," "don't end up in a ditch," "be calm and gentle at the wheel," "don't over react to the strange manoeuvres of others"—all brilliant advice. Secondly, and far more importantly, pétanque is like business—which brings me to the story of my first two-on-two, "team versus team," match.

Occasionally others were also playing in the darkness on the same soil that we were, which was also part of my schooling: how to play with other matches going on around you; and how to apply the appropriate etiquette needed to ensure you didn't interfere with other guys and yet weren't so passive as to allow others to bully their way through your match and impact your concentration or timing. One night there were two gentlemen of roughly my age (mid thirties) playing alongside us. I recognized them as off-duty local policemen—a pair of *gendarmes* who regularly performed critical security roles, like enforcing the driving regulations that only permitted Saint-Pauloise (residents) with special permit cards to drive within the walls of the ancient town.

Preventing outsiders from driving within the walls of the ancient town actually was necessary and important. When I first chose Saint-Paul as the charming French village I would call home for my stay in France, entry by car was controlled by a barrier arm that was triggered at night by cards with magnetic strips that the town issued to residents. Yet during the day the barrier was raised and real live police were stationed at the gate to check cards and wave drivers through; I can only guess that during the day unscrupulous tourists would try to follow the cars of locals before the barrier could descend, making it necessary to utilize two highly paid and armed human beings to control daytime access. (Incidentally, I am certain that any tourist who managed to sneak a car inside the walls of the town must have regretted it within milliseconds of discovering the intimidating reality that its one-way ring road was like a not-quite-circular bowling alley with irregular vertical stone walls on both sides. And making matters worse, that locals drove this ring road at close to the speed of the Monaco Grand Prix F1 race without touching their brakes, even in the narrowest sections that offered only a finger-width between one's side mirrors and the stone walls on both sides, and that they would not hesitate to lean on the horn if anybody was doing otherwise.)

For some odd reason, maybe a misguided attempt to save money or to free up the *gendarmes* for more satisfying assignments, one day a construction project started to remove the barrier arm and replace it with something more high-tech that would not require human babysitting during daytime hours. The pétanque grounds outside the Le Café de la Place offered the perfect vantage point to discreetly observe activity at the barrier. The construction of the new system wisely started in the fall, after the summer waves of tourists had subsided, lessening the odds of glassy-eyed pedestrians being crushed by a backhoe operated by a heat-stroked operator dreaming about his upcoming summer vacation. As we continued to play our game while our metal balls grew colder and colder in our hands with the change of seasons, we watched the project for several months, finding it hard to fathom the need to dig a hole, fill it in, dig another hole, fill another hole in, repeat, repeat, repeat.

When the grand project was complete and testing had begun we finally could see that a bollard, a short stout vertical post like those installed to protect the US embassy entrance in Paris from an oncoming tank assault, had been installed in the middle of the narrow road. Residents would swipe a magnetic access card past the new device that looked as fancy as a BNP Paribas bank machine a few metres before the bollard, which was oddly positioned to force the driver to move across into the wrong side of the road to reach it (no comment). A few seconds after the swipe, the bollard would begin its graceful piston-like descent below ground level, where it would stay for about 15 seconds or longer if a car was on top of it. We looked at each other, shrugged our shoulders and *puffed* out air, which meant "Interesting, let's see how this plays out."

The first month the system went live was my last month living in Saint-Paul, so I didn't get a chance to see how the project that took longer to complete than building the Paris Metro worked out. It was only when I returned for a visit a few years later that I saw that the bollard had been replaced with a barrier arm just like the one that had been there before, which pretty much told me all that I needed to know about the conclusion to the drama that we had observed in that first month of testing—a mixture of comedy and tragedy. Most residents would swipe their cards and then speed forward for fear the bollard would attack them from below, sometimes spinning their tires and laying rubber in their haste. Less clever drivers would struggle with the timing of the card swipe and the descent and reappearance of the bollard.

The worst example I viewed in person back in the testing phase was a gentleman in a gorgeous sports car who triggered the bollard descent and then took his time putting his card back in his wallet before driving forward. By the time he got moving the bollard had begun to rise, but the forward movement of his sparkling, sexy, Italian car, which had him seated very low, prevented him from seeing its re-emergence from its subterranean lair. A large number of the locals playing pétanque (me included) or seated in the café saw what was coming and yelled "*Arrêt!*, [Stop!]" but apparently the cool character behind the wheel must have thought we were screaming because we wanted a photograph of him and his car, so he didn't touch the brakes until the massive bollard had done the braking for him—*crrrrunch* was the sound I recall, followed by cheers, jeers, and catcalls from the assembled audience, who seemed to have been waiting for just such an entertainment bonus for months. The car was a mess. The bollard descended as if trying to hide from a pending second punch and then returned a few seconds later with no signs of being any the worse for wear.

But back to the pétanque ground and our gendarme opponents. There was zero interaction between these two cops and us, as they played their game against each other, and Hubert and I played ours. It was on this night that I first defeated Hubert in a very close match—and it turned out that this would be my last one-on-one match against him and therefore my only win over him ever, because as soon as I defeated him he declared, "You are ready."

"Ready for what?" I asked innocently.

"You and I are going to play as a team against *les gendarmes*," he replied very matter-of-factly.

I wasn't prepared for this sudden announcement and found it difficult to remain calm, and appear like I was ready and not sensing the onset of incontinence. I was afraid of letting Hubert down and being the cause of us going down in defeat to the policemen, maybe so badly that we would both have to kiss the Fanny. Later I came to see that this surprise declaration of our first match against another team as another example of Hubert's clever way of teaching a rookie to play pétanque—information provided on a need-to-know basis, so as not to overflow the student's head or allow him to think about future subjects that would only undermine his ability to practice and apply the lessons being taught.

Hubert waited for the policemen to finish their match and then approached them quietly, I assumed so they could decline quietly if they preferred not to play a mixed-doubles team of one Frenchmen and one Canadian. As he walked back to where I was patiently and nervously waiting, a subtle grin came across his face. When he reached me he said quietly, "We play; you will be the *pointeur*, don't make a *putain d'merde* of this."

As if I wasn't anxious enough about how I would perform and whether or not I could figure out how to play in a complementary manner with my first teammate—being the *pointeur* while he was the *tireur*. His slang-infused directive made me shake in my dusty sandals, *putain* being the English equivalent of the F word and literally meaning "whore," and *merde* meaning "shit." So *putain d'merde* is a complex combination of these two very common French swear words that can have several translations, which I will leave to you to imagine, though which I understood to be a harsher version of something like "Don't f**k this up in a messy, smelly way for me."

It turned out that the two teams were very well matched and it required a time-consuming back-and-forth battle to reach a victor in this best-of-three-games, slow-moving, humidity-infused competition. Hubert couldn't really coach me too much as the match progressed—well he could have, but he certainly didn't want to show any sign of weakness to *les gendarmes* that would lift their confidence and give them a mental edge. So I had to read his facial expressions, body language, and exhalations for cues as to how we were doing and how to behave. You would think the score was enough of an indication of how we were doing, but not so.

This is where I come back to pétanque being a metaphor for business. Just because you are struggling or succeeding at one particular moment in time does not indicate that the same will be true when the game reaches its climax. The challenge is long, so staying with your strategy is critical, not showing frustration is important, and not becoming over-confident or complacent is a must. Working for a struggling high-technology start-up in a foreign country, completely on my own, I was experiencing all of these things in business on a daily basis, though I really didn't pause often enough to consider them and how they were affecting my life, my state of mind, and how well I was doing my job—oddly, pétanque and Hubert made me reflect on this, which over time made me a stronger businessperson.

This match was the first in which I heard two phrases pass Hubert's typically sarcastic lips; both being pieces of deadly serious, sage advice that will stick with me for the rest of my years in many facets of life. The first is "Limit the loss,"- meaning, when things are going badly, you need to pull back from being aggressive, limit your losses from getting worse, lick your wounds and live to fight another day. In our game that evening it really meant that if it appeared that we were not likely going to win one round, that wasn't the end of the world as long as we made moves to ensure that the other team only scored one or two points, rather than three or four or even five or six that would spell a disaster from which recovery of the match would be unlikely. Whenever Hubert could tell that I was pressing and thinking about attempting a high-risk shot without the match being on the line, he would lean in towards me and whisper, "Limit the loss." I would then eat my pride and play safe shots to restrict the damage for that round.

The second phrase is about doing exactly the opposite: "Sign the contract," meaning close the deal when it is on the table; seize the opportunity when it is ripe for the picking; don't let an opportunity slip through your fingers; force them to sign the deal when you have leverage; go for the jugular, right now. When Hubert could see me hesitating to attempt a daring shot that, if executed well, would turn the tide of a match or extend our lead to one that was practically insurmountable, he would again lean in and very quietly yet forcefully whisper, "*Signe le contrat.*" He knew that I would then feel more at ease about attempting a gutsy shot, and hopefully would pull it off. I rarely heard him utter the phrase, so, when he did, it never failed to set a fire in my belly and I typically nailed the shot, much to the pleasure of my mentor, whose eyes were the only part of his body that would give away his extreme pleasure—they would grow wide and bulge out for a split second and then quickly return into his head without anyone except me noticing, indicating what I am sure was a thought something like, "Holy crap, he pulled it off again; *pas mauvais pour un petit canadien* [not bad for a little Canadian]."

In our back-and-forth battle with the *gendarmes*, we won the first game by the required two-point minimum, 13–11, in a little over an hour. They showed no fear and won the second game in an even longer marathon than the first game, 15–13. Nobody was there watching; nobody knew the significance of this match to me, the foreigner who had been trying to break into this charming piece of French culture for months. Yet it felt to me like the entire country of France was watching, cheering for the two off-duty policemen, hoping they would send the little Canadian packing back to his home country after this, his first and last pétanque match, with his grand total of wins being zero.

Something changed in the third and decisive game and Hubert and I somehow caught fire as teammates and took control, winning without nearly as much tension, 13–7. The most magical part for me was that I got to deliver the game-ending points on one of those shots where Hubert whispered "*Signe le contrat*." It wasn't the most challenging ball I rolled through the darkness that evening, but it wasn't straightforward either—I had to bowl my ball around one of theirs that was blocking the path to the *bouchon* and park it close to another one of our balls that was sitting closest to that little target, thereby scoring us two points and ending the game, and the match at two games to one. As my ball clattered across the sand and pebbles in the dark of night, avoiding the ball blocking the way to victory and then gently curving and slowing to a stop within inches of the *bouchon*, I wanted to jump out of my shoes, do a fist-pump, and yell so loudly it would be heard all the way to Nice.

But somehow the subtle glare delivered to me by Hubert, as it became clear that the ball was going to stop in a victorious position, told me not to do anything hasty and to follow his lead—a firm squint of his eyes and eyebrows and a gentle nod of his head, told me "Job well done, contract signed, be calm." So I followed him over to shake hands with the polite policemen. In my eyes, we had just vanquished them in an epic battle lasting nearly three hours, though to them I believe it was more like just another match that didn't quite go their way and that provided a nice break for two friends to relax in each other's company after a long day at work. We shook hands and only uttered "*Bon match*" to each other, and then parted ways without any fanfare.

I had wanted Hubert to tell them I wasn't a local; I wasn't even French; I was Canadian; I had only lived in France for six months; and this had been my first official match—but he did no such thing. He turned and said to me, "To the bar for a drink."

As we walked side by side, I said, "I want to high-five you and jump up and down."

With a look of disdain in his eyes, he replied, "We don't do that; we don't celebrate victory that way," and kept walking to an open table on the terrace of the café. It started to sink in for me that this was a game that involved honour and that if you played it for a lifetime, often with the same opponents, you didn't gloat about winning or take losing too hard. The respect you gained from winning came as much from understanding how to win with grace, as being skilled at the game itself—once again, very much like the world of business and in fact, life in general. Though don't get me wrong; Hubert was delighted, which could be seen on his face and in the way he walked with a slight bounce in his step—he was delighted that he had been able to teach a raw rookie how to play this complex game well, and to win the first match he had played with his eager student. The way he went about enjoying this delight very quietly and with humility over a glass of pastis was frustrating to me at the time. Though once I could reflect on it, I felt inspired just a few hours later over breakfast alone in my funky cave apartment, as I gazed out over the 14th-century medieval ramparts of the village and the maritime alps of the Côte d'Azur in the hazy, humid distance.

That morning I arrived to my French lesson with teacher Colette both excited and exhausted from lack of sleep. "I played and we won," I blurted out.

"*En français si vous plâit,*" ["In French, please."] she replied.

"*J'ai joué et nous avons gagnés* [I played and we won]." I responded, surprising myself at how quickly I could say this in French without thinking hard.

I suppose it was the fire in my eyes, combined with her years of wisdom, that enabled Colette to know immediately what I was talking about, so she said *"Felicitations, je suis impressionnée* [Congratulations, I am impressed]." We spent the entire hour-long French class conversing in French about the past night's events, which forced me to tell the story slowly and made it easier for her to absorb despite my highly excitable state that was a poor match for her calm personality.

The next time we met for another lesson, a week later, Colette told me that she had shared my story with all her friends and they had found it a wonderful tale. I wasn't sure if that meant they thought it was a great achievement or a cute fairy tale, but it hardly mattered—it simply felt nice that she had felt compelled to share it. Maybe at long last I was starting to have my first breakthrough into experiencing French culture as a live participant, rather than as a passing observer, as had always been the case since my first visit to the country some ten years earlier as a young university graduate on vacation. I couldn't stop smiling as I left that French lesson and walked back to my car—smelling the sent of Mediterranean flowers that was a constant presence all summer long, and allowing the thought of starting-to-fit-in to wash over me.

7

GO BUY BALLS

T HE NEXT time I bumped into Hubert after our ground-
breaking victory over the *gendarmes,* and its valuable
lesson in how to celebrate a win with class, there was
an assignment in store for me. He told me that now that I
had a team victory under my belt, it was time to go purchase
my own set of balls, so that I no longer looked like an ama-
teur who had to borrow a set of balls from a café barman.
He added that I would come to understand over time how
important a role psychological advantage (i.e. mind games)
played in matches, and that it was critical that I do everything possible to exude confidence and expertise, which
included arriving on the pétanque grounds with my own

private ball set. He went on to emphasize the importance of this assignment by sternly telling me that he would not play in the light of day with me as his teammate, until I succeeded in procuring a set of balls that were appropriate for my style of play and physical stature. When I asked for some ball-buying tips, Hubert only scrunched up his face, delivered me a sharp *puff*, turned, and walked away. I actually felt flattered that I was being ordered to go spend some of my hard-earned francs on three metal spheres that were held in such high regard by so many Frenchman. What I failed to realize was that I was also being ordered to spend a half-day of my hard-earned leisure time and to put my newly acquired broken-French skills to a test.

The shopping assignment turned out to be far more challenging than I had expected, as was just about every other first-time task in France. To start with I had to find the nearby town of Vallauris and its Obut store—smartphones with GPS and Google Maps not yet invented, so I grabbed my trusted Michelin map and off I went down the A8 *autoroute* that I had become quite familiar with in the opposite direction towards Nice, but had never driven west towards Cannes on. Incidentally, I would only learn later that Vallauris was one of the towns that Pablo Picasso had lived in, when he had spent time living, painting, and sculpting on the Côte d'Azur.

By now I had become well accustomed to driving in France, including navigating both large complex roundabouts and tiny versions of those tricky circular intersections that we don't have in Canada. The best advice I can offer a foreigner confronted with these circles-of-confusion for the first time is to pretend you are like a horse with blinders on—consider anything you cannot see to be behind you and thereby forced to yield to you; if you flinch and turn your head a little to let more objects come into view, you lose, and will likely never get out of the roundabout until you incorporate this methodology into your driving style. I found Vallauris and the Obut store without much trouble in my sporty rental Renault Mégane without being honked at even once. After I'd parked half on the sidewalk, where a parking-prevention bollard had been knocked down to open up a perfectly viable parking space, I strolled confidently into the shop to take care of what I thought would be a ten-minute stint of shopping—just the way I like my shopping trips.

The brand Obut is probably as well known in France as Nike—the go-to name for pétanque balls, made and designed since 1955 in the tiny picturesque town of St-Bonnet-le-Château. I couldn't resist visiting their website, before I set out on my trip, and loved how they described their philosophy: "Sunshine, nature, family, good friends, a good-humoured spirit and healthy competition: these are the values of pétanque on which Obut has built ... to last." I could tell I was going to enjoy the shopping assignment!

As I pulled up to the Obut store, I was surprised to see that from the exterior it was a nondescript building with a couple notable exceptions: one shiny, metallic, three-foot tall *pétanque* ball and a one-foot tall *bouchon* adorned the front steps—balls that Goliath of Gath would have had fun playing with if David had challenged him to a game of *pétanque* before vanquishing him with a slingshot. The moment I entered the store I was overwhelmed by the variety and magnitude of the stock of ball sets—it looked similar to an old-school shoe store that stacks shoeboxes to the ceiling on every wall. I was welcomed by a woman in her fifties named Geneviève, who I quickly learned either spoke not a word of English or who had immediately sized me up, by my foreigner pronunciation of "*Bonjour*," as a target for some good laughs to liven up an uneventful day. Geneviève looked and behaved like she currently had inquisitive grandchildren that it was her duty to teach much about French culture. Despite the language barrier my poor French created, she was very patient and seemed to genuinely enjoy educating me about the nuances of a facet of her country's history. After a few awkward minutes of introduction, which started with me announcing, "*Je suis ici pour obtenir des boules* [I am here to obtain some balls]," we got down to business. I suppose my naiveté about the complexity of the pending task, and the fact that I must have seemed like more of a tourist than a resident, led Geneviève to begin by taking me to the museum portion of the facility for an introduction to the history of the game and the evolution of its balls.

The small museum was impressive, featuring glass showcases that housed displays of old balls and famous matches. Of course, most of its content was lost on me, though I could appreciate the care and pride that had gone into developing it. One exhibit that did fascinate me showed how the first balls had been made entirely of wood from the roots of boxwood bushes (the wood being durable and commonly used for carving or turning small objects like chess pieces, musical instruments, and door handles). The exhibit also showed how over time forged nails were added by hammering them into the wooden balls to improve durability, creating what were called *boules cloutées* [nailed balls]. A wide variety of designs and patterns were created by using nails of different colours and metals (steel, brass, and copper), sometimes resulting in genuine works of art that are valued by collectors today. Many months later, I spotted and purchased one such remarkable-looking nailed ball at a weekend market in another small village of the region—the ball still sits on a shelf in my den, alongside the set of modern balls that I would purchase from Geneviève that day in Vallauris.

She explained that in the sixth century BC the ancient Greeks had played a game that involved tossing stone balls, which the ancient Romans then modified by adding a target that had to be approached as closely as possible; I wondered what the ancient Greeks were tossing balls for if there was no target to aim at, though I didn't understand the origin of Olympic sports as discus, shotput, and javelin, so I let her continue without interrupting with a sarcastic question. The Roman variation of the game was brought to Provence by Roman soldiers, and by the Middle Ages was known as *boules* [balls] and was played throughout Europe. It is said that King Henry III of England banned the playing of the game by his archers because he wanted them to be practicing archery, not boules—though I suspect it was because he heard the French were enjoying the game and getting good at it. In the 14th century, Charles IV and Charles V of France forbid commoners to play boules, a ban that was only rescinded in the 17th century—I suppose the Scientific Revolution of that century brought the freedom to throw spheres in parabolic arcs without applying for royal permission.

By the 19th century, the game had evolved into lawn bowling in England, while in France it was still known as boules and was played throughout the country. In the south of France, it morphed into *jeu provençal* [game of Provence], similar to today's *pétanque*, except that the playing area was longer and players ran three steps before throwing the ball. Apparently this jeu provençal originated in the town of La Ciotat, in Provence, close to Marseilles and less than 200 kilometres from my home turf of Saint-Paul de Vence.

Geneviève explained that the name *pétanque* comes from *petanca* in the Provençal dialect, deriving from the expression *pès tancats*, meaning "feet fixed" or "feet planted" on the ground—or in modern French, *pieds tanqués*. She also mentioned that a boules event, involving two versions of what today is pétanque, was a demonstration sport in the 1900 Paris Olympics—two matches were played, involving 13 players (all of them male); France won both, mostly because both matches featured France vs France. When I looked this up online later, I discovered that ballooning, cannon shooting, pigeon racing, kite flying, and angling were also demo sports at those Olympic Games—I am not being facetious; this is factual.

I was interested in this history lesson from an expert, though as a strong saleswoman and good judge of the male attention span Genevieve sensed when my eyelids were growing heavy from information overload. So she turned off the encyclopedia-like fountain of knowledge, and took me back to the showroom to examine this year's line of shiny metal accoutrements.

As I glanced around the room, I realized I was in way over my head and would need a lot of help from this knowledgeable woman. There appeared to be a mind-boggling array of options ahead of me—my brain equated the showroom walls and aisles stacked with boxes of different balls to a maze of women's dress shoes stacked up in a Galéries Lafayette department store—it nearly made me comatose. Geneviève jumped in with the first important question to help narrow down the selection process, asking if I was a *pointeur* or a *tireur*.

Of course, I was proud to be able to answer this without hesitation, replying emphatically and with a playful grin, "*un tres bien pointeur.*" She took my hands in hers, examined them closely, and then caressed the entire length of my arm, as if she was about to kiss me deeply—yet she only muttered a few words, which I think meant something like "rather small and soft due to too much time working on a computer, though surprisingly strong." She then explained that she was selecting for me a magnificent set of balls that were 71 millimetres in diameter (appropriate for my small hands); 710 grams in weight (fairly heavy and appropriate for my strong arm); level 115 hardness ("half-soft" and I didn't care to know why); solid stainless steel (I suspect because I gave her a budget that did not lead her to the fancier metal alloys that would require a bank loan); had a fairly complex striation pattern (I understood, rightly or wrongly, that this was to aid in gripping the earth if I was to put spins on the ball during my *pointeur* duties); and that they were referred to as a "competition set," as opposed to a lowly "leisure set" (she must have been able to tell by my fierce intensity that I was no mere recreational player). She pointed out that every set came with a *cochonnet* and a small cloth for dusting one's balls, all in an elegant leather carrying bag that would become the first and only purse-like object I would ever own.

I thanked Geneviève for her outstanding level of patience and assistance, and proceeded to proudly pay with my credit card that was issued by the Banque Nationale de Paris, which to me was a sign of French citizenship because it had been harder to qualify for than a Canadian passport. I tried to hide my surprise when the number that came up on the cash register display was more francs than I made in a week, pulling my bulging eyes back into my head quickly and then keying in my security code as my hands trembled. Hiding the excitement of believing that I was about to successfully complete my Hubert assignment, I calmly strolled away from the cashier with my heavy little purchase tucked under my arm. As I exited the building, I noticed a quote on the wall that read "*La pétanque... c'est comme un soleil qui se point!* [Pétanque is like a ray of sunshine]." This metaphor resonated with me, and I smiled deeply while turning to wave goodbye to Genevieve, as she bid me "*Bonne chance* [Good luck]."

The drive back to Saint-Paul seemed like a slow-motion dream. I couldn't wipe the ear-to-ear grin from my face as I twisted and turned my way back into the hills above the Côte d'Azur, a local radio station blaring the latest French techno hits, the heat and humidity hardly noticeable despite the normal trickle of sweat down the middle of my back. I imagined that Geneviève would go home and recount a tale of having sold balls to a curious Canadian who somehow was playing pétanque in, of all places, Saint-Paul de Vence, and that her awestruck husband, after a sharp exhale *puff* of air in her face, would have emphatically said something like, "You must have not have understood the terrible French of the Canadian because there is no way that a foreigner could be playing pétanque in such a wonderful French town."

As I reached my village, I waved with a newfound confidence to the *gendarmes* manning the haphazard barricade system at the village entrance, this time thinking to myself, "Now I have really arrived in this fantastic town and I am finally ready to become a part of its pulse."

8

WHAT'S A VERNISSAGE?

THE DAY of my successful ball-shopping excursion, I got home in time to intercept Hubert just as he was about to leave for a social event. When I waved in the air the shopping bag that contained my purchase—actually sort of swinging it as I held it high, since it was far too heavy to wave—Hubert smirked at the accomplishment of his pupil, who had crossed another bridge by managing to successfully purchase pétanque balls, all on his own. When I opened the bag, and then the yellow and blue cardboard box with the famous Obut logo on it, he was quickly able to confirm that my purchase was at least somewhat appropriate for use by a teammate playing on the terrain of Saint-Paul de Vence. Not just any balls would have received his blessing for play on the same soil where such French icons as Yves Montand had played. After humouring my excitement for a few minutes, Hubert changed the subject by saying, "OK, enough of this; we have a *vernissage* to attend."

"*Qu'est-ce qu'un vernissage* and are you saying I am invited?" I replied.

Out came that all-too-frequent look of disgust and disappointment on Hubert's face, which occurred whenever I demonstrated that I did not know something that he felt every human being on Earth should know from birth. A *vernissage*, he explained with an air of superiority in his voice, is a preview of an art exhibition before its formal opening, and this one would be a private affair that I could attend because I was a friend of his. He told me to hurry to get cleaned up and make myself presentable, so that we could leave at once for a gallery only a hundred metres away, which was owned by a friend of his. I darted into my cave to freshen up and reemerged within minutes, eager to experience another element of French culture yet unknown to me.

As we walked, Hubert managed to further intimidate me by explaining that the *vernissage* guests would be served *canapés* (another word that he had to explain to me) and wine, as they discussed the works in the exhibition with artists and others who possessed a deep knowledge of art. So when we arrived and I was introduced to the hostess, I politely accepted a glass of wine and quietly tagged along with Hubert as he mingled and introduced me to all sorts of colourful locals, who engaged me in conversation despite my bastardization of their language. After we had consumed a couple glasses of wine, Hubert said, "You know you should drink more often, your French improves with each glass . . . and if I drink too, then it's a lot less painful for me to listen to you speaking my language."

I had a lot of entertaining, and likely partly misunderstood, conversations and interactions that fine evening, as I tried hard not to let my incredibly deep pit of cultural ignorance show through my polite exterior. When I approached a Camembert cheese plate, I started to panic, realizing that I had never really known if one was to eat the waxy exterior or only the soft centre. Back at home in Canada I wouldn't have worried about what anybody thought, and probably would have only eaten the inside, but here I felt like discriminating eyes were watching. So I served a stranger a slice of the cheese and watched him eat it, the entire slice, before I dared to advance on my portion with my teeth. I only learned years later that the outside is not wax at all, and actually a rind that is formed naturally from the mould that is sprayed on during the cheese-making process. Thank goodness I didn't say what I was thinking at the party, which was, "Hey, are you supposed to eat the weird-coloured wax on the outside or not?"—which of course I couldn't have figured out how to say in French anyway.

I met many interesting locals that evening, though only one who became a true friend over time. His name was Pierre and he was the coolest, best-looking, suavest guy I have met in my life to this very day: tall with dark Mediterranean looks, perfect swept-back hair, just a hint of a stubbly beard that made him look tougher than he probably was, and sharp casual clothes that included a sweater draped over his shoulders on a hot night, which somehow didn't make him break a sweat... oh, and boat shoes that he wore without socks every single time I saw him throughout my entire year in his country. He seemed to be a charmer of all the ladies and the envy of every other man in the gallery. This guy's warm smile, that made him ridiculously good looking whenever he flashed it, charmed even me. He made me think of the word *debonair*, which I had only heard in a few movies—I even looked up its exact meaning the day after and it fit: courteous, gracious, with a sophisticated charm and a carefree and cheerful manner. I got the impression that he was wealthy and maybe even from aristocratic bloodlines, though I would learn later that this was not even remotely close to the case, which turned out to be a nice surprise. When Hubert introduced Pierre to me, he said, "*Ah oui, Monsieur Obut,*" which was absolutely hilarious and clever in my eyes, and which told me that he must be a close friend of Hubert's because he had already been informed of my successful shopping excursion and was likely aware of our sordid pétanque tryst.

Because this *vernissage* was a preview of an art exhibition, there were many other local gallerists present. Giselle, a sixty-something woman, was very fashionably and yet modestly dressed, and always made time for me in her gallery to talk culture and generally assist me with my slowly improving French. I often thought that she must have been a stunner in her youth and always enjoyed our conversations, which had an odd air of flirtation about them given our age difference. After I had been introduced to Pierre and our initial conversation ended, Giselle came over to me and, while looking him up and down, said to me in French, "Pierre always looks so good in Jean Paul Gautier prêt-à-porter fashion, does he not?" The first thing that went through my inside voice was, "A hockey defenseman went on to become a fashion designer? (Jean Gauthier played professional hockey in the '60s and '70s.)" Fortunately, my outside voice simply said, "Ah *oui, il le fait* [Oh yes, he does]," and thankfully the conversation ended there because it was already making me uncomfortable watching the way she undressed him with her eyes.

Also in attendance were Henri, the wine connoisseur and sommelier, who always gave me great local vineyard tips; big-man Louis, whose gallery was full of provocative massive sculptures and bronzes that made me blush; Simone of the souvenir shop and her gorgeous young daughter Sabine (whose mother's eyes told me "Don't even think about it, mister"); and Renée of the modern art gallery, whose beautiful works I couldn't afford. They were all polite and relatively engaging, which surprised me and provided the encouragement I needed to continue my quest to break through into a few elements of French culture.

I wouldn't say that Pierre and I became the best of friends over time, but we certainly developed an odd connection that surfaced a few times over my year in Provence. I say "odd" because he spoke no English (or so he had me convinced) and I was never entirely sure if our discussions in French were mutually understood all the way through or not, and because we didn't seem to have a lot in common—me being a high-tech Canadian from a large city and he being an artistic Frenchman from a small town.

The most memorable time we spent together came one morning soon after the *vernissage*, in the framing shop that he owned and operated in Saint-Paul. On a cycling trip in the Luberon Valley, I had acquired what to me was a fine piece of art depicting a summer vista in Provence, though it was actually little more than a glorified poster of an art piece, and I wanted to have it framed. I visited Pierre in his shop early one weekday morning. I had intended to select a frame with him and then return to my office to do some serious work that morning, never expecting that a session with Pierre early in the day could involve needing a nap by 11 am. He dropped what he was working on when I walked through the door and completely focused on assisting me with choosing a frame, mat, and glass for my poster, without every once making me feel unimportant. As he laid out many creative colour and style options in front of me, we discussed work, life, women, and sport. About a half hour into the process, which I had expected to be wrapped up at that point, he asked if I wanted to join him in a glass of pastis. He probably felt, like Hubert did, that speaking with me completely in French was more pleasant when partially inebriated.

I thought 9 am was a bit early for a drink, but it would have been rude to turn him down, so I agreed. With the slight of hand of a magician, he produced from a shelf below the counter a Ricard bottle about half full of the licorice-tasting liquor, two glasses and a pitcher of ice water—how civilized! And so the banter gradually became more lively, the belly laughter more frequent and deep, and the balance more challenged. During one story about a wonderful woman, he referred to the lovely lady as "*un petit cadeau* [a small gift]," which he explained meant that she was a beautiful little gift that one should tie a bow on, love and keep safe. As he provided this explanation he made motions with his hands of slowly tying a ribbon into a bow on a small box—quite possibly the most romantic description I had ever heard, and one I imagined would be much more powerful if told to a special woman over a glass of wine in a nice restaurant. Somehow in the midst of the stories and the laughter we managed to finalize the details of the framing, and by about 10:30 Pierre put up the Closed sign and he and I staggered out in the bright sunlight—the actual framing, the setting of the price, and the payment to occur at some undetermined time in the future. We shook hands and he wished me a good day, "Bonne journée Monsieur Obut," and I went home to my cave and fell onto the bed for a couple hours. Where Pierre went for the rest of that morning was none of my business, though in my head I imagined that he must have dropped in on a young lady friend's place nearby.

My adventurous day of pétanque ball shopping had been topped off nicely by learning what a *vernissage* was, making a new friend, and stumbling home to drift off to sleep pickled and content—the staggering home to be repeated soon, due to my new friend Pierre's early-morning workshop hospitality.

9

BECOMING A RIVERAIN

HAD NOW secured my first team victory, played in a clandestine manner under the cover of darkness, and successfully procured my own set of balls. With these accomplishments to my credit, Hubert informed me that I was finally ready to play in broad daylight with him daring to be my teammate in plain view. This of course implied that if I made him look bad, he would be risking the scorn of his townsfolk—*les riverains*. Now I never actually heard anybody refer to anybody else, or themselves, as *riverains* of Saint-Paul de Vence, but after discovering a sign near the entrance to the village that read "Sauf Riverains," I became enamoured with the word and used it to give myself a chuckle from time to time.

Charles the baker found me amusing, not so much because I was actually funny, but because I was an odd curiosity to him as a rare foreigner living in his tiny town. His bakery was, of course, one of the most important parts of local village life and was open each day long before any other shop within the walls of Saint-Paul. Though I typically stopped by only to purchase a baguette, the shop's wares included a tantalizing collection of goodies like *pain au chocolat* [a croissant with chocolate baked inside of it]; *croque monsieur* [open-faced sandwich with ham and melted Gruyere cheese]; sweet and savory crepes made fresh, while you watched; and best of all in my books, *tarte tatin* [upside-down caramelized-apple pie that had so much butter and sugar in it that it should have been law that the vendor have a heart defibrillator on the premises]. One day when I was visiting his bakery to buy a steaming-fresh baguette for breakfast, he remarked that because I was secretly learning to play pétanque, I was really becoming a "local"—so it seemed that Hubert had shared our little secret with a few friends, or that it was being leaked by the *gendarmes*, who we had so soundly defeated in the dark. I responded emphatically, "*Oui, un riverain,*" which brought a puzzled smile to his face.

"*Un riverain?*" he asked.

I explained that I had seen a do-not-enter sign that read "Sauf Riverains," and that my French teacher had explained that the sign meant that only locals should enter... though I still didn't understand exactly how the word *riverains* translated. Charles laughed out loud so hard I thought he was going to split his apron wide open and explained that the word was ancient and meant "a person who lives by the river," to which I replied, "But there is no river here."

He laughed even more loudly and said, "Very well, you are a *riverain* of Saint-Paul!" From that time on he greeted me with "*Bonjour Monsieur le Riverain.*" I didn't mind if he was poking fun at me, since I really had asked for it, and because he always smiled when he said it and I had no issue with being the butt of an inside joke if it brought a smile to a fellow *riverain*'s face.

Being about to step into the light from the cover of darkness, by graduating from playing pétanque only at night to playing during the day, brought to mind some of the many Marc Chagall pieces that I had seen in galleries during my time in France. Living in Saint-Paul de Vence was in many ways like living inside an art gallery, or maybe more like being a part of one of the works on a gallery wall. The ancient walled village with its narrow cobblestone alleys, wide variety of unique window shutters and doors, spectacular array of flowering vegetation and stunning vistas, can make you feel like you are living within a painting of one of the great modern masters, only better because you can also sense the aromas, tastes, sounds, and *joie de vie* of the inhabitants of the south of France.

And then there were the small, classy, beautiful galleries that lined the narrow pedestrian streets of Saint-Paul. I spent a lot of time wandering into these unique, colourful places, which were often owned and operated by equally unique and colourful lovers of art. During these gallery visits, I would try to learn something new, practice my French, and simply enjoy absorbing the qualities of the collections that were displayed. Over time, I gradually developed loose personal friendships with several of the gallery keepers. I say "loose" because although these relationships often grew to include a genuine fondness and interest in one another, they were confined to the galleries and did not extend into life outside of the shops, and unfortunately their development was often limited by language barriers that stunted their potential.

One of the gallery keepers, who seemed to enjoy speaking with me in French and encouraging the development of my grammar and vocabulary, connected with me in a relaxed and seemingly familiar manner. Adele was in her mid 60's, and married to a painter, whose work adorned the gallery that she managed. Her warmth and kindness reminded me at times of my grandmother Eve, back when I was a kid and she was a great storyteller who loved to laugh. One day when I remarked that a painting in Adele's gallery reminded me of a work by Marc Chagall, she asked me if I realized that Chagall had lived and painted right here in Saint-Paul for much of his life. At first I thought I had misunderstood her because of my poor French comprehension, though when what she was explaining became clear to me, I felt embarrassed to be so uneducated about art and history. When I said, "*Vraiment? Ici, à Saint-Paul?* [Truly? Here, in Saint-Paul?]," she replied, "*Bien sûr, et il est enterré ici dans le cimetière* [Of course, and he is buried here in the cemetery]."

I was stunned that I had inadvertently chosen to live in the French village that Chagall had called home for years, and in which he had created many of his most famous works. He had lived here from 1966 (the year I was born an ocean away in Ottawa) to 1985. During that time he relentlessly incorporated the village and its ramparts into his paintings, which often depicted couples in love and multi-coloured bouquets swirling above the village in a serene Mediterranean sky.

I was further surprised that I had been living in this village for several months completely unaware of this incredible piece of local history. When I asked, quite embarrassed that I had to, if Chagall had lived his entire life here, Adele replied, "Non, il était un Juif russe" [No, he was a Russian Jew].

I responded without hesitation, "*Comme ma famille* [Like my family]," and was amazed to hear her immediate response, "*La mienne aussi* [Mine too]." So we did share a connection that explained the comfort of our interactions, despite the challenge posed by not sharing a common language.

I typically visited Adele's gallery weekly to have a warm conversation about some element of artistic technique or art history. During one visit, I managed to reinforce both my art and French history naiveté. Actually it was worse than being just naïve, and more than being uncouth too. A better word for my lack of knowledge on these subjects would be *philistinism*; luckily for me there was nobody around with long hair named Samson to have a stern talk with me. My own grandmother Rachel was the only reason that I had even a little appreciation of and understanding for art. When I was a child, she had taken great joy in enticing me to meet her for trips to Canada's National Art Gallery in downtown Ottawa, by offering to buy me grilled cheese and French fries in the cafeteria (an aside: it now occurs to me how silly calling them "French" fries is, particularly since the French call them *pommes frites*). She would focus my art education on the work of Canada's famous Group of Seven and on Emily Carr, who painted vibrant landscape scenes of our beautiful country, and also on collections that featured French artists, such as Renoir, Matisse, and Monet. Granny Rachel would always take time to show me with detailed motions of her soft, aging, thin hands how the brushstroke techniques of each of the artists differed. Finally, this tutelage was paying some dividends as Adele tried to teach me a few things about French art.

When Adele pointed out that Pablo Picasso had also spent much of his life in the south of France, living a short while in and around the nearby villages of Golfe-Juan, Antibes, Vallauris (where I had gone to buy my pétanque balls), and Mougins (where he is buried), my philistinism made its first appearance of the day. I blurted out without much thought, in my broken French, "*Ah oui, le français qui a peint tout dans des formes étranges bloqués* [Oh yes, the Frenchman who painted everything in strange blocky shapes]." The look on her face quickly changed to stern, as she tried to politely give me an education, rather than a scolding, saying, "*Picasso était espagnol, pas français, et la technique dont vous parlez est le cubisme, qu'il a inventé et qui n'a pas été le seul style de sa carrière* [Picasso was Spanish, not French, and the technique you are referring to is Cubism, which he invented and which was not the only style of his career]." Gulp. I smiled with a squint, and said, "*Je suis desolé, merci pour l'éducation* [I'm sorry, thank you for the education]." Gulp, smirk.

Appropriately, she then assigned me the task of visiting both the Picasso Museum in Antibes and the Chagall Museum in Nice. I was fascinated by both eye-opening experiences, and the highlight from both was soaking in the details of Picasso's lively, playful, cubist piece *La Joie de Vivre* [The Joy of Living], featuring a nubile girl dancing and playing pipes with other merry creatures by the ocean. Its light-hearted happiness comes back to me whenever I am exposed to French art.

I always left Adele's gallery to return to my work feeling a little more cultured and a little lighter and more relaxed inside. Was this due to Adele's kind manner, or due to having learned something new, or due to gradually feeling like I was melting into the culture of the region and its people?

As I started to say my goodbyes at the end of one visit, I mentioned that I wouldn't be around for a week or so because I was headed to Jerusalem for the first time in my life, on a business trip. Adele's smile grew from ear to ear and she eagerly told me that she had a son living in Jerusalem, who also worked in the technology industry, and who had a wife and infant son. She insisted that he and I connect and that he and his wife would be pleased to have me over to their home on the outskirts of Jerusalem. She also asked that I take a small package of gifts for them that she had been intending to mail.

When I said that it would be a pleasure to meet her son and his family, Adele didn't waste any time, grabbing her phone to call him right then and there. After a few excited words in French with her son Daniel, she passed the phone to me. Daniel was equally as welcoming and charming as she was, and the fact that he spoke English made it possible to have an efficient phone conversation that I could be sure I was interpreting correctly. So I was set; I now knew somebody in Israel other than my business colleagues, and I would deliver him a package from *grand-mère* and have a nice evening with him and his family.

When I landed at Ben Gurion Airport and made my way to see the infamously high-security Israeli border control staff, I was initially very at ease—until the conversation with the first officer started! I should mention that the Israelis do not handle airport security like most—they believe that far more can be understood about a person and their intentions by having an in-depth conversation with them and reading their body language, than by ripping apart their baggage and asking only simple questions. And so it started, not with the expected "Why are you visiting Israel?" or "What is the purpose of your business in Israel?", but rather with questions meant to surprise and that might even seem personally intrusive in many other places, such as, "Welcome to Israel, are you Jewish and do you have family here?," and then, "Did you speak to anybody in the past few days about visiting Israel?"

When I replied "Yes," "No," and "Yes," with explanation of course, since the questioner's tone made it abundantly clear that each question should be answered with some explanation if one was wise, my answers lead to a pause and then a friendly, "Tell me more about this person who you spoke with about your upcoming trip to Israel and have you known this person for long?" My mind started racing. I completely trusted Adele and knew there was nothing to fear, yet I also knew that my next few answers were not going to result in a quick passage through security control and on towards a taxi to my hotel, and maybe instead to an interrogation room and a sleepless night.

"Well, you see, I have been living in France for a few months and met this woman who operates an art gallery and she has a son who lives here, so we talked about my trip . . . ." Gulp.

"That sounds like a very nice experience, Sir; will you be meeting her son here?," continued the young officer.

"Oh yes, he works in high-tech like me, and we spoke once over the phone, and I will be meeting him for dinner a couple nights from now..." Gulp.

"Isn't that nice that you have a new friend to visit in Israel. By any chance were you asked to bring or send anything to him, and if so, what?"

At this point I felt the blood rush to my cheeks and away from my brain and heart, and started to feel light-headed, as the officer looked over his shoulder and nodded towards a back room, after which another officer joined her and politely introduced himself. I then stuttered and stammered, "Um, yes, his mother gave me this package to deliver, and I didn't ask what was in it because she said it was mostly gifts for her grandson." I then pushed the small box towards them in a manner that was intended to deliver the message that I didn't mind if I never saw it again and they were free to blow it up if they wished; that I was sorry for having been so reckless and potentially being a naïve patsy; and that I was really close to staining my shorts.

The first officer said, "I'm sure there is no issue, but can we please open the package and inspect it together?" My head-nodding was eager and rapid, and when we opened the package to find some photos, letters, and a bottle of jam that easily could have been something much more nefarious than a bottle of jam (though I was absolutely sure it wasn't), I nearly passed out.

"Please wait here for a few minutes while we inspect your jam," Officer Number One said, and then she disappeared into a back room and left me with Officer Number

Two. I tried to smile innocently and added, "You know, it's not MY jam; it was given to me." This generated the first stern facial expression I was to see and resulted in no further conversation from Officer Number Two for a full three or four minutes, which seemed like hours, as we awaited the return of his somewhat kinder colleague. She eventually came back with a smile on her face that I construed as either "You are a numbskull, but are free to enter Israel and have an enjoyable stay" or "You have the right to remain silent..."

Now I am not a religious person, but afterwards I gave thanks to God that it was the former and that I was handed back my now chemically tested jam and a somewhat disheveled package for delivery to Adele's son, and sent on my way into Israel. My dinner with Daniel and his family a few nights later was a delight and we had a good laugh at my story, as he apologized for his mother putting me in such a precarious position, when she could have easily mailed the small package for a few francs and avoided the drama for me.

And somehow Israel wasn't finished dishing out odd experiences to me. The next time I visited the country I travelled with our new local sales rep, Neshar, who was an ex-fighter pilot in the Israeli Air Force, not your typical background for a high-tech salesman. As we started to drive from our hotel in Tel Aviv towards Jerusalem, where the day's meeting was to take place, Neshar took a phone call in Hebrew. I don't speak much Hebrew, but based on the frustration in his voice, the sudden change of direction of the car, and my knowledge that there was only one highway between Tel Aviv and Jerusalem, I attempted to calmly interject, "Hey, we aren't driving to Jerusalem."

When Neshar got off the phone, he said, "There is a traffic problem, so we are going to fly to Jerusalem." I knew we weren't driving towards Ben Gurion Airport, so I blurted out in near hysterics, "Do you mean YOU are flying us to Jerusalem?" The one-word answer was "*Ken,*" which means "yes" in Hebrew, and which made my eyebrows raise as high as they could go up my forehead. Off we were to a nearby airstrip with a one-room office, where Neshar signed out a Cessna from a pool of small planes, after which I watched him check the little plane's fluids and then helped him to push it out from under the roofing that protected it from baking in the near-desert sun.

As we flew, wearing headsets, Neshar explained the precise altitude corridor we had to maintain to fly in the crowded Israeli airspace used by small private planes, large commercial planes, and a wide variety of military jets and helicopters. I asked if it was the West Bank below and if rifles could reach our altitude... "*Ken*" and "*Ken*" were the answers.

I hardly recall that day's business meeting because my brain was in shock from the surprise flight in the smallest plane I had ever climbed into, over the most fought-over land I had ever flown over, and consumed with processing the fact that we still had a return flight to survive. Both short flights that day were beautiful and nerve-wracking experiences, and I was never so happy to land on a runway and walk away from a plane as when we touched down back in the Tel Aviv area and tucked the little plane back into its parking spot.

I am not very well read about the personality of Marc Chagall, though I have to surmise that if his spirit had been watching my Israel escapades, he would have been at least amused. Had I not stumbled onto my ethnic connection with art gallery keeper Adele, I might not have then stumbled onto the fact that Chagall had lived in the same village in France that I was living in, a village I had accidentally stumbled into when arriving from Canada. Had these accidents of chance not occurred, I would not have experienced the colourful, stumbling, misadventure of my first arrival into Israel, which I will be recounting for the rest of my life. And though the Cessna flight experience from my second trip to Israel had absolutely nothing to do with Chagall, I imagine that it too would have tickled his spirit to watch me stumble my way through a few words of Hebrew and have my heart skip beats at the hands of an Israeli fighter pilot turned computer chip salesman, whose name meant "eagle."

I can never think back on my Saint-Paul time without images coming to mind from Chagall's works that depict figures hovering peacefully above the ancient, rampart-guarded village. Those souls apparently absorbing the colourful beauty below them, and probably the scents and sounds as well. And to think that I had even just a little something in common with Marc Chagall, outside of our heritage—that we had both been riverains of Saint-Paul de Vence at one time in our lives—adds yet one more element to my everlasting fondness for the time I spent soaking in life in the south of France. Maybe, just maybe, Chagall was now a permanent apparition hovering above Saint-Paul, smiling down as I had lived through my little adventures there.

I cannot capture in words my gratitude for the time I was privileged to spend in this part of the world any better than Chagall himself did, when he wrote, "I thank destiny for leading me to the shores of the Mediterranean."

10

STEPPING INTO THE LIGHT

NOW THAT I was the proud owner of my very own set of pétanque balls, complete with a rag for cleaning dust off them, a *cochonnet* (target ball) and a leather carry bag to tote the kit around with style and confidence, I went to Hubert to ask him when we would play next. In typical Hubert fashion, he was non-committal and abrupt, sniping, "When I have time and the moment is correct, I will retrieve you." That stung a bit and felt as though I had become an object to bring along to the playing grounds, much like my new ball kit.

And this is pretty much how it always went being Hubert's teammate; that is to say that, as the far junior member of the squad, I had absolutely no say as to when or who we would play. Match times seemed to spring up almost without warning, requiring me to either drop everything to play "*maintenant . . .* at once" or miss the opportunity and likely not get another chance for several days. And so I waited for our inaugural daylight match to be sprung on me, and waited, and waited some more. The undefined waiting period was actually appropriate, given the refreshing pace of life of the south of France, where many businesses still paused a couple hours for the midday equivalent of a siesta, and where waiters still could be heard walking away from you after announcing "*J'arrive!* [I'm coming!]."

And then the big moment finally did arrive! I would emerge from the shadows and play pétanque in the warm sunlight of Haute Provence. On not just on any old pétanque grounds, but on the old hallowed grounds at Le Café de la Place in Saint-Paul de Vence. Grounds that movie stars like Yves Montand and Simone Signoret, heads of state, and royalty had graced with their presence, just before they strolled across the street to savour fine food and champagne at the famous La Colombe d'Or. The moment came with a loud thudding series of knocks on the heavy door of my cave-like Saint-Paul apartment. It was Hubert, and when I opened the door he said with a devilish twinkle in his eye, "Grab your balls, let's go, we play now!"

As we walked together down the sweaty-tourist, crowded, narrow, windy, cobblestone alleys of the village, not a word was said between us. Hubert did his usual muttering of tourist insults in French, while bumping these cash-spending, bling-wearing, sunburned, folks aside with soft yet effective body checks that made the Canadian hockey player inside me proud that he had learned something from my influence. Hubert kept his pétanque balls behind the counter at the café, like a real *riverain*. I carried my new set by the handle of its leather bag, which somehow didn't feel to me like a man purse, though it surely must have looked like one to the tourist throng. I could feel that I had a swagger in my step and was conscious of it being a bit over the top, but I had a hard time eliminating it from my gait because of the weight of the very solid set of three metal balls hanging off one arm. Hubert's shaggy, aging sheep dog, Enzo, and I followed his lead-blocking all the way to the dusty patch of dirt in front of the café. (Enzo was named after sports-car maker, Enzo Ferrari—he sure wasn't speedy, but he could weave through the pedestrian tourist traffic of Saint-Paul with the best of them). Hubert's march seemed modeled after a peasant leading an uprising at the start of the French Revolution, guiding his troops into battle, brimming with confidence as he pushed forward without hesitation. Bringing a foreigner to play pétanque risked painting himself as an outlaw, though if his forces could gain respect, he might be seen as some sort of rebel leader eventually.

Once our motley militia of three navigated the sea of tourists and arrived at the pétanque grounds, my eyes started to scan the edge of the pitch for a pair of teammates who appeared to be waiting for opponents to arrive. And then I saw them: it was my debonair, zero-English-speaking new friend Pierre and another *bon vivant* about ten years my senior, who was looking very serious or maybe annoyed because he had been roped into being part of the

first opposition to face off against the ragtag team of Hubert and Le Petit Canadien in broad daylight. His name was Maurice and the look on his face conveyed that he knew no good could come of this. Should he and Pierre defeat Hubert and me, as expected by every single French soul who might catch wind of this travesty, they would be teased for even having been drawn into such a farce and thinking it had been honourable to drub a foreigner and his misguided French tutor. On the other hand, *mon Dieu* and heaven forbid, should they somehow manage to lose to the little foreigner and his imprudent local coach, he would so regularly become the butt of jokes that cut so deeply to the bone of his Frenchmanliness that he might have to emigrate to someplace terrible like England or Canada.

I shook hands with Pierre and we exchanged a few pleasantries in my broken French that always made him cringe his facial muscles in a way he couldn't disguise. He then introduced me to Maurice, who also appeared to speak no English, and who feigned a brief smile that I read to deliver the message, "I am going to embarrass you so badly that you will never want to play again in my country, and then I am going to make my teammate and your silly friend buy me drinks all afternoon long for having subjected me to this painful affair."

As we readied to play, I noticed that there were several other matches taking place on the pitch. I had of course observed this phenomenon before, but had never played in the midst of it, since night play never generated a simultaneous match count of greater than one. On the pétanque grounds of Saint-Paul, matches being played at the same time were not organized in structured parallel lines so as to completely avoid the others' space, as I had witnessed in other locations. Instead, the direction of play was a free-for-all that respected common courtesy, yet that ebbed and flowed throughout the match and caused games to be intertwined without actually going so far as to cross paths. It was a delicate dance with no words ever spoken between matches about where each proceeded from one round to another and only rarely involving even a close-call between the balls of different matches. And the field of play was irregular in shape to begin with and contained a couple very large plane trees, whose roots buckled the soil and caused miniature dry river valleys to form and reform after each rainstorm.

The realization that I was now playing in primetime, which implied all sorts of new nuances to adjust to, did ruffle me, and I could feel my pulse quicken as Hubert let me make the throw that determines which team will start with the advantage of throwing second. One player on each team throws one ball at the *bouchon* and he whoever gets closest wins the right to start the match by tossing the bouchon and then having his opponent make the first throw at that target. My nerves got the best of me and Pierre easily won that advantage and proceeded to start the match by tossing the bouchon into one of the little dry river valleys quite far from where we were standing—and sadly for me, that was to foretell how the match would go. Based on Hubert's rather *laissez-faire* reaction after we were disposed of in two straight games (recall that a match is a best-of-three competition), I knew that my play had been respectable and not brought embarrassment to him, which at least signaled that my *boules*-playing career was not going to be cut short after Day One of being permitted to play while the sun was in the sky.

Our losing scores were 13–6 and 13–10, which Hubert pointed out to me quietly afterwards were not even close to "Fanny kissing" territory and which didn't give Pierre and Maurice anything to boast about. Maybe the outcome was actually perfect—it took my confidence down a notch and taught me that I still had a ton to learn; it neither humiliated our opponents nor gave them reason to dismiss me as unworthy of playing in Saint-Paul; and most importantly, it maintained my friendship with my coach and encouraged him to continue with my tutelage. We retired to the café for a pastis, bought by Hubert, likely because he needed to thank his friends for being willing to play us and for being polite along the way and after the fact. Most of the conversation excluded me, simply by being at a pace too fast for me to keep up and on subject matter with which I wasn't familiar. This allowed me to quietly sip my pastis, while eating roasted nuts and ruminating on the fact that I was sitting with three Frenchmen on the terrace of an ancient café in Provence after having somewhat successfully participated in my first real match of a game near and dear to their hearts.

WAS I FINALLY arriving within France, after having lived there for several months already? It felt like it, and the subtle glow about me certainly must have shown.

11

MIND GAMES

HAD ARRIVED in France back in January and the hands-on portion of my pétanque education had begun in the darkness of the chilly evenings of winter's short days. As the scents and colours of spring took hold on the Côte d'Azur in March, so did my determination to solidify the right I had earned to play during daylight hours under the watchful eyes of my neighbours. Typically, Hubert and I would match up against pairs of men who were relatively close to him in age, which meant they were five to ten years my senior and had twenty-five or more years of pétanque under their belts. We came up against many different local pairings, and sometimes complete strangers who were on vacation from Paris or other parts of the country. The outsider teams were far easier prey because they didn't possess local knowledge of how the micro-geography of our sandy, uneven, tourist-infested grounds played.

My favourite team to play was the always-entertaining dynamic duo of Rémy and Jean-François. Rémy was a mystery to me because he seemed to pretty much live at the café and on the pétanque grounds. He wore ratty jeans and usually an even rattier t-shirt, was never clean-shaven, his hair was usually disheveled, and he regularly smelled like a blend of whisky and old socks. I wondered how he made a living and imagined that, based solely on the bags under his eyes, he might be a night-shift worker at a nearby parfumerie, or at the port of Marseilles, or maybe at the Nice airport. Or could it be that he was independently wealthy, having made a fortune as an art dealer, jeweler, or currency trader? When I discreetly asked friends about Rémy's lifestyle, I got a far less glamourous image painted for me. It turns out that due to the generous nature of France's social safety net, Rémy had become adept at ostensibly being a blue-collar worker holding down a number of part-time roles in a variety of trades, though actually being a professional at being unemployed nearly full-time. This lifestyle seemed to wear quite well on Rémy and one would think that, given the amount of time he spent playing boules, he should be a regional champion. He was indeed a skilled player and I became fond of him and his colourful personality, though he had one very over-developed Achilles heel—a complete lack of mental toughness. This characteristic, alongside his very dramatic and oftentimes circus clown-like comedic mannerisms, made him and his teammate Jean-François fun to be around on the pitch and to play against. J.F. was the quiet straight man of the team and Rémy the boisterous, emotional yang to his yin.

My mentor, Hubert, was also a skilled player. Where he differed the most from Rémy on the playing field was in his mental approach to the game. Hubert always carried with him a devil-may-care attitude that reeked of sarcastic wit and abruptness, which he could transform in an instant by layering on charm when it served him well. He was unflappable and didn't change his outward demeanor during any phases of a match, no matter if we had a large lead, were mired in a close battle, or were in the midst of being trounced. He taught me this skill and, moreover, how to play mind games with opponents who were clearly susceptible to being derailed mentally, though they might be just as good or better, technically, than we were. And he regularly made comparisons to the business world and life in general, to show how mental steadiness and toughness are important everywhere. Poor Rémy (I say that with the fondest of memories for the man) was ripe for being picked apart with mind games on the days when his physical game was at its best, and even more at risk of losing to us on days when he was hung over or especially tired and lacking physical sharpness too.

One classic technique I would employ to begin the process of setting Rémy off, which I pulled from my quiver of somewhat-dirty tricks only when I felt I needed an extra edge to put us over the top, was to exclaim after I made a decent shot, "Wow… *je suis seulement un débutant!* [Wow… I am only a novice!]." That one simple line, delivered with a pause after the "wow" and a look of puzzlement on my face, was like touching a cigarette to a short fuse connected to a large stack of dynamite on Rémy's back. Smoke billowed forth immediately, followed by a massive explosion within seconds! I used this line at least once a month, to the point where you would think that Rémy would grow immune to it over time, but he didn't. The magic word was débutant [novice], because it cut so deeply to be threatened with defeat by a little guy speaking poor French who was a newbie to France, Saint-Paul, and pétanque.

If you have strong mental fiber, you simply recognize the attempted mind game, chuckle right back and move on, mostly unaffected. Rémy, instead, would typically toss his cigarette to the ground, let out a big exhalation of smoke, and begin a tirade that I always had to work hard not to laugh out loud at. It would go something like, "*Merde* [shit], *ce n'est pas possible* [it isn't possible], *ce n'est pas vrai* [it's not true], *ce doit être un rêve* [this must be a dream], *putain* [whore], *bordel* [whorehouse], *putain d'merde* [f-off]." In a bit of a twisted way, it would make me churn inside with delight. If I looked Hubert in the eyes while it was going on, I would have to turn my back to him quickly and walk the other way to prevent myself from letting out an infectious bout of laughter. I would stroll around in a small circle to regain my stoic facial expression, before returning to the epicenter of the explosion. Delivering this line was usually good for at least two to five points over the next few rounds, and sometimes it ate at Rémy for so long that it was all we needed to gain the upper hand and ensure that victory would come at the end of the multi-hour match.

Now the "Je suis seulement un débutant" mind torment was just one weapon at my disposal. Keep in mind that all the good players had their own verbal weapons locked, loaded, and ready for deployment, and these varied so widely and were so creative that it really took a lot of fortitude not to be rocked by them at times. One afternoon, one such bomb came from such an unexpected direction that it rattled me. It wasn't that the verbal dig upset me, rather that it was so hilarious that I couldn't get beyond it for several minutes, which made me lose focus during that time.

We had played a winning first game in a match against a couple of solid players, and then, for some inexplicable reason, I lost my touch and went cold in the second game, making uncharacteristically bad shot after bad shot for several rounds in a row—yes, it happens to even the best of us high-performance athletes. A weathered old local, who played often and quietly watched from the edge of the grounds even more often, clearly knew who I was and had a good sense for how I played. I had never heard him utter a word; he just watched with his arms folded and smirked from time to time without ever passing comment. Yet on this day, he couldn't resist the urge to blurt out a zinger when I missed a very easy shot, the latest in a long string of misses. His interjection was like a blindside tackle in football; I didn't see it coming and it stunned me badly and left my ears ringing and my chest hurting for several minutes due to the gut-wrenching laughter it provoked inside me.

Without warning, immediately after my bad shot stopped rolling, he snapped out just two words with strong emphasis from his perch several steps behind us: "Canada Dry!"

It nearly dropped me to the dirt; whoa, that was clever and funny, and 100% unexpected. It caused Hubert to make a guttural noise from gulping in a mouthful of air that he hadn't planned on inhaling during the normal course of breathing, which only amplified its impact on me. I still don't think the older gentlemen was cheering for our opponents or meant any ill will towards me; he just couldn't resist letting his clever thought out of his cranium, and was probably curious to see if I had the fortitude to absorb it and rebound. I laughed loudly, gave him a nod and a wink to show how much I appreciated his wit, then tried to dry my eyes so I could carry on playing. We made the game close, but I never regained my form completely and we lost the match, though I would never credit his jest for any part of that loss, of course. So the verbal mind games can even come from the peanut gallery. Watch your back!

To further spice up the potential for mental anguish, the verbal mind torture can be creatively augmented with a vast array of physical techniques that also cause mental pain. I prefer to refer to these techniques as "strategy," rather than mind games, since that sounds much more sporting. Here are some illustrations of a few of these little grenades (recall that to tire is to shoot at an opponent's ball by throwing your ball through the air, and to point is to roll a ball along the ground gently).

When your team has earned the right to toss the bouchon for the new round, you may toss it so that it lands anywhere between six and ten metres from the throwing spot. If you know the preferences of your opponents well, you will throw the bouchon close or far depending on how those preferences match up to your own.

Another rule when tossing the bouchon is that it must not come to rest closer than one metre from an obstacle like a tree or a rock wall. Though the rule says nothing about letting it come to rest in a dry river valley caused by rain runoff or the little sandy river deltas that grow at the end of such rain features, and some players absolutely detest playing close to terrain features like these.

A fundamental premise in pétanque is *"boule devant, boule d'argent"* [a ball in front is a money ball], meaning that a ball located in front of the bouchon is much more valuable strategically than one located behind this little target ball because it blocks the opposing team from easy access to the bouchon. Should a team place a "money ball" so closely in front of the bouchon that it will be difficult to place another ball any closer, then the tireur could opt to throw directly at the bouchon, to try and remove it completely from the playing area, thereby nullifying the round completely and forcing it to be replayed. Nothing upsets players more than when they are almost certain they have a high-scoring round set up nicely, only to have the bouchon punted miles away by a well-aimed tire.

Refusing to get in a rut or a predictable pattern of play can also trigger disorientation among the opposing team. At each opportunity to be the tosser of the bouchon, if one has the mental metal to choose a slightly different position on the terrain and then to be unaffected by the changing surface, the other players will soon be in awe of your ability to handle any and all conditions and will most certainly gradually lose their focus. A well-timed verbal joust as soon as the bouchon arrives in a sandy spot, after having been in a firm location the round before, such as, *"Ooo, sur la plague, après avoir été sur la route* [Ooo, on the beach, after being on the road]" can help exacerbate the decline.

And then there is the act of "measuring," which is often necessary, though seldom used as a strategy to gain advantage, except by unscrupulous players the likes of Mabel the Rule-Bender. (Of course, I only called her that in my own head and privately to Hubert.) Mabel was my least favourite person to play against, female or male. She played fast and pushed others to play that way too, which always made me feel rushed and typically resulted in me playing poorly; this was her number one mind game and it worked, which I admit is why I didn't care for playing her. To her hurried pace of play, she added a hurried use of her measuring tape. Whenever it is hard to tell which one of two balls is the closest to the *bouchon*, somebody pulls out a tiny measuring tape or a small roll of string from a pocket to accurately assess which is the better ball. Once one player from each team concurs, the ball that is further away is pushed aside by one's foot to indicate the decision to all. Well, not quite with Mabel; she would whip out her measuring tape, make a very quick measurement of both balls and then, before anybody else could get near enough to view her measurements, pronounce her decision and kick away the loser ball so quickly that no verification of her officiating could be made. This drove me nuts and a few times I tried to argue, but she would just give me a dismissive and scolding shush-be-quiet type of gesture and sound with a finger to her lips, before turning her back on me and walking away to start the next round. As you might imagine, my ball was never deemed the closer ball in any of Madame Rule-Bender's measurements. It was only over time that I came to realize that everybody else humoured Mabel's cheating because she wasn't a terribly strong player and they had some sympathy for her. Regardless, I preferred to beat her, though we rarely managed to do so, and when I would start to get upset, Hubert would motion to me in a manner that conveyed the message, "Be calm, it means nothing to us, and a lot to her."

I IMAGINE THAT somewhere in pétanque lore there lies a story of a legendary player who must have once uttered something similar to the great New York Yankees' baseball player, Yogi Berra's, famous line, "Baseball is 90% mental and the other half is physical."

12

NOT SO LOST IN
TRANSLATION

As WE played during one so-hot-it-was-hard-to-move
afternoon, I couldn't help but overhear the conversation
of a retirement-aged couple from what sounded to
me like the north of England. They were trying to figure out
how this odd pastime with metal balls was being played.
Standing just off the edge of the grounds, they couldn't even
tell which players were playing against which players, just as
I had struggled to determine the previous winter when I had
sat watching. I had become aware during the middle of the
summer that tourists watching from the café saw me as part
of the scenery, part of what made this village so picturesque.
This revelation warmed my heart each time I noticed the

eyes of tourists intently watching matches in which I was an integral part. But it wasn't until listening to these two searching for the keys to unlock this game that an epiphany took root. It suddenly hit home how ingrained into the woodwork of this facet of Saint-Paul culture I had become, and just how much I was going to miss being a little knot in this ancient tree someday.

After listening to the couple guess incorrectly about the ins and outs of the game for nearly an hour, I decided it was time to help these frustrated folks understand the basics. I didn't want to let them return to England messing up yet another piece of French culture, by delivering an incorrect explanation of the game to friends over a bangers-and-mash breakfast. Without turning to address them where they stood, just a couple feet behind me, I said quietly, "Sorry, but you are mistaken; we each have three balls per round, and the order in which we throw them is only determined after the result of the previous round." The wife let out an overly dramatic little gasp and replied, "You speak English without an accent; you aren't from here." Luckily the urge from the nascent Frenchman part of my brain to reply with "No shit, Shakespeare," was overridden by the overly polite neurons in the still healthy Canadian part of my brain, and I said, "Correct; I am Canadian and I've been living here for a while."

A barrage of questions followed as the couple looked down into their Lonely Planet guidebook, shocked that their little travel bible seemed to be inaccurate. I did my best to answer them when I could between throws, and when I also could do so quietly and discreetly enough to avoid the wrath of my fellow players, who I knew didn't really care for educating tourists, especially English ones. Hubert eventually noticed what I was doing and under his breath said to me, "Tell them to go read up on *Jeanne d'Arc* [Joan of Arc]." I, of course, knew the name (sadly, mostly because there is a major boulevard in Ottawa named after her, which always gets mentioned in the news on the radio due to traffic congestion, rather than because I am a little bit worldly). Hubert then whispered me a brief education in French that caused me to have to hide a chuckle.

My translation of his whispered mini-rant is, "Joan of Arc helped to recover France from English domination during the Hundred Years' War and she was eventually captured by the English and burned at the stake. Tell them that we have not forgiven them, and if they keep annoying us by asking ignorant questions, we will warm up the fire pit behind the café and they can join us for a roast. Oh, and also tell them the only way to endure summer in England is to have a photo of summer in Provence framed and hung on a wall in a comfortable room." The last part of the insult I looked up later because I found it so clever; it turns out Hubert borrowed it from Horace Walpole, an English historian and politician from the 18th century, which made his quoting it all the more ironic and hilarious.

Part of me wished that I had never let on that I wasn't a Frenchman who either couldn't understand them or preferred to ignore them, though a bigger part of me enjoyed explaining the highlights of the game right in the midst of a serious match. This made me feel like I was so ingrained and so expert in this game that I could now serve as a spokesman for it without my fellow players feeling the need to stop me. That said, I never repeated this tourism service because I found it quite tedious and very distracting to my play. Hell, it turns out that pétanque is really hard to teach to spectators, never mind novice Canadian players. No wonder that nearly a year ago Hubert had greeted my request for tutoring with that classic French *la puff* exhale and frown.

WHENEVER I WAS going to have to pack up and leave this place, I was really going to miss its laidback people and this wonderful, dusty, hard-to-understand pastime. I was going to miss so many things about the south of France that I had thought to be quirky or annoying when I had arrived, yet had grown to understand and sometimes even appreciate over time. Like French service and the fact that it is OK that it doesn't typically come with the same level of insincere butt-kissing that is deemed normal in Canada and the U.S. Many would summarize French service as "rude"; frankly, it often is, though usually that is only because the French don't suffer fools easily, speak their minds, don't sugarcoat things, and don't apologize for things that are out of their control.

Because I had to leave and re-enter France roughly every second month to give the appearance to the French authorities that I wasn't working and living in France, and was just a tourist who loved France so dearly that each time he got home, he did his laundry and returned a few days later, I had to pick up a rental car at the Nice airport every time I flew back in from Canada. I only ever saw two different Hertz employees and I know they came to recognize me, yet neither woman let on recalling ever having seen me before.

Maybe they just did their jobs without imprinting anything that seemed to be useless information, and probably only would serve to replace what was truly more valuable information; things like knowledge of red wine and the perfume scents of the wide variety of flowering plants of the Côte d'Azur.

Over the span of two successive trips to the airport during the middle of my year, I felt like I had lived within the French version of a memorable Seinfeld episode from 1991: Jerry's interaction with a car rental agency employee, which went like this...

Agent: "Sorry, we have no midsize available at the moment."

Seinfeld: "I don't understand; I made a reservation. Do you have my reservation?"

Agent: "Yes we do, unfortunately we ran out of cars."

Seinfeld: "But the reservation keeps the car here. That's why you have the reservation."

Agent: "I know why we have reservations."

Seinfeld: "I don't think you do; if you did I'd have a car. See, you know how to take the reservation; you just don't know how to HOLD the reservation, and that's really the most important part of the reservation, the holding; anybody can just take 'em."

Agent [after returning from speaking with a manager]: "I can offer you a compact car instead of a midsize. And would you like to take the insurance?"

Seinfeld: "Ya, you better give me the insurance because I'm gonna beat the hell out of this car!"

My French version from 1999 started with me returning
to the Hertz counter at the Nice Airport for what must have
been the 4th time that year, tired from the long trip from
Vancouver to London Heathrow to Nice, and it went like
this...

> Agent: "Votre nom [your name]?"
> Paul: "Paul Shore."
> Agent [as she scans the list on her computer screen for my
> name]: "Monsieur Sho-re, Monsieur Sho-re, Monsieur
> Sho-re, ah oui, voila, Monsieur Sho-re... we have no
> car for you." (The South of France, Italian-influenced,
> accent leads to my name being pronounced in two sylla-
> bles in a very pleasant sounding manner: "Show-ruh").
> Paul: "Ah, excusez moi, no car?" (as I think about the Sein-
> feld episode, though I am too tired to point out to her
> that 'holding' the reservation is much more important
> than 'taking' the reservation).
> Agent: "Let me see what I can do... hmmm... ah, an
> upgrade is possible, from your Renault Mégane to a
> Renault Espace."
> Paul: "Magnifique, merci!"

And so, after the usual delay for paperwork that stopped
just short of asking your blood type and political views, off I
trotted to find my Renault Espace, the parking lot pavement
so hot it was becoming soft under my shoes. When I got to
the parking spot noted on my paperwork, a short couple of
hundred metres from the terminal building, I was disap-
pointed; no, I was downright pissed off to find out that the

model named Espace, *meaning space*, was a minivan. What the hell! I was a single guy living in a town whose one street was so narrow a motorcycle felt like an overly large vehicle choice for navigating around it—I didn't want a minivan for two months! But I was jet-lagged, sweat-soaked, and not willing to drag my bags back across the molten parking lot to the back of the Hertz line only to be told something like "*Je suis desolé monsieur*; if you don't like the Espace then I suppose you are walking," so I threw my stuff into the cavernous cargo area, slammed the massive hatchback closed, sped off home, and swore to myself for two months for being such a wimp, as I drove much more slowly inside the village and struggled to park every single day.

I was a very happy man when the two months were up and I had to fly back to Canada as part of my ongoing immigration ruse, and I flipped the Espace keys to a puzzled-looking Hertz agent as I said, "*Merci pour l'Espace, plus jamais* [Thanks for the Espace, never again]."

When I returned a week later, I thought I was surely done with this Seinfeld-esque episode in my life, but I was wrong...

Agent [the same woman as the time before]: "Votre nom [your name]?"

Paul: "Paul Shore."

Agent [as she scans the list on her computer screen for my name]: "Monsieur Sho-re, Monsieur Sho-re, Monsieur Sho-re, *ah oui, voila*, Monsieur Sho-re... we have no car for you, but I can do for you an upgrade to an Espace."

Paul [raising my voice and not even trying to start in French this time]: "No, no, no, no way. Last time I was upgraded to an Espace and I had to put up with being a single guy driving a minivan in Saint-Paul de Vence for two months. Do you know Saint-Paul? Can you imagine how terrible it is to drive that car there for two months? Or frankly how terrible to drive a car like that just about anywhere in the south of France, where I have seen even those cute little Smart cars parking sideways to invent a parking space for themselves? I will stand here until you give me the Renault Mégane that I booked or something similar in size and quality."

Agent: "Very well Monsieur, let me see what I can do."

She then typed and searched and typed and searched for several minutes, at which point the German tourist who was behind me in line boldly stepped around me, bumped me aside, and joined the fray:

German tourist [in a stern and sarcastic manner]: "Mademoiselle, I am only going to be in France for a week."

Agent [glancing up over top of her reading glasses and smirking]: "Well then, Monsieur, I guess it is going to be a week less a day."

And then she went right back to looking down at the computer and searching for a solution for me. "Wow, stronger French resistance than during World War II," I chuckled politically incorrectly to myself. After about ten minutes she found me a comparable Peugeot, I assume by messing up the "reservation" of some other poor person who was still in the air on the way to Nice.

This type of "lost in translation," or at least "lost in culture," experience was another aspect of life in France that I would one day miss too.

FROM TIME TO time, I would notice that these sorts of interactions had gradually started to leave a mark on my psyche that exposed itself through changes in my behaviour. The start-up I was employed by had its world shaken up when our largest partner, Texas Instruments, up and acquired our number one competitor in the summer. This huge American computer chip maker had its European headquarters located on the outskirts of Nice. This was the reason we had opened our European operation in this area, and now they were going to own a competitor of ours, so it was pretty clear that my days in France were now numbered.

The day the unsettling news broke, my parents, Zelda and Steve, just happened to be staying with me, after spending a few days in the Luberon Valley. We went to dinner in the nearby seaside town of Antibes, where Picasso had worked for a few months in the grand building that is now the Picasso Museum, only a block away from where we were dining outside in the steamy heat. During dinner I casually remarked, "Either our little company is dead and I'll be back home in Vancouver soon, or something great is going to happen, and I'll be back home in Vancouver soon." The very matter-of-factness of my statement was a clear indication of the calming effect living in this part of the world was having on me, and it did not go unnoticed by my folks, who knew me to be a high-strung and easily wound-up type.

Good news was soon to come, though; the acquisition triggered a domino effect in which major computer chip companies all rushed to find new dance partners, small software companies specializing in Voice over IP applications. Our company got caught up in the buying spree, just as Texas Instruments was casting its old girlfriend aside for its surprise new wife and leaving us cast adrift. The company that acquired us was Californian semiconductor powerhouse Broadcom and they quickly integrated me into their European sales force, reporting to a fantastic Dutchman with a *joie de vie* attitude I came to love. This put a happy ending on a tech start-up story that could well have ended tragically. By the fall, I had agreed that a better long-term role for me lay back in Vancouver in a marketing job running a chip group, and that I would wrap up my work in Europe by year end and return home.

While the acquisition was still being negotiated, our founder quietly told me what was going on and when it would become official; yet the day when he called an all-hands meeting to announce the deal to all the staff was still a special one for me. It was August and almost unbearably hot and humid in my little Saint-Paul cave, where I set up to dial in to the conference call because it was already evening my time. I sat shirtless at my tiny kitchen table, wearing only my underwear as sweat trickled everywhere. I was of course in a jovial mood because I knew what was about to be discussed, though I didn't yet know what it meant for my future in France, much less my career.

When I joined the call and heard my thirty-or-so colleagues on the line back in Vancouver, we exchanged a few sarcastic boy-I-wonder-what-this-is-about jokes as we waited for the founder to walk into the room. I had prepared myself the exquisite meal of a baguette and a couple cheeses, plus a bottle of cheap, yet decent, red wine. I finally tired of waiting for our boss and decided to pull the *bouchon* from the bottle, but neglected to mute the phone. When the ensuing "pop" of the uncorking echoed around the inside of my cave, the line went silent and after a pause the cofounder asked, "Was that a cork?"

Uncharacteristically I blurted out, "Yep, and I'm sitting here in my underwear waiting for this meeting to get underway." Despite how important I knew the meeting was going to be and how much a lot of the people in that room looked up to me as one of the leaders of the group, I couldn't help from spontaneously being smug, entertaining, and raw with the gang—hmmm, it seemed France really had rubbed off on me; actually, it had really gotten into my bloodstream, just as the red Bordeaux was about to. A roar of laughter came blasting through the crackly speaker of my home phone, and just as it died down the founder entered the room back in Vancouver, so I never did have to comment more about doing a team meeting while drinking in my undies.

This change in demeanour and self-confidence must have had something to do with the influence this country and its people had been having on me for a little over half a year. And the change didn't come only from life in Saint-Paul playing pétanque. Another source of influence came from some of the young Frenchmen (and French women) with whom I worked and socialized.

My best friend in my age bracket was a kind-hearted young woman named Sophie, who seemed to recognize my need for companionship (platonic that is) and regularly invited me to join her and her friends on outings. Weekend trips to the Maritime Alps with Sophie and her friend, Monique, were a fun way to relax and put my French to the test. One such day, I snowboarded while they skied, and during a pause on the hill I peeled off a layer of clothing and said, "*Je suis chaud*," which I thought meant "I'm hot," as in "I'm too warm and need to take off my jacket to cool off." My two cute young lady friends fell down laughing in the snow, and after catching her breath, Sophie said, "Oh, you think you are, huh?" and then went back to laughing. Eventually she managed to explain that the correct phrase would have been, "*J'ai chaud*," which indicates that you are overly warm rather than "hot," as in sexually attractive.

I had also become close friends with a product manager named Gerard who frequently entertained and amazed me with the depth of his wit and style. I regularly met him at his tiny apartment in the old part of Nice for a night out on the town. The first time I went to meet up with him, he told me I could find his pad by walking the main pedestrian street and buzzing the door behind "the snake guy." He wouldn't explain what this meant, but when I saw a man painted completely in silver doing performance art with a boa constrictor, also painted in silver, wrapped around him, I knew I had found the place. Gerard's apartment was Spartan—it had a sofa, a CD player, a piano that he could play well, a bed, a table with two chairs, and a fridge that contained only several half-bottles of inexpensive champagne and plenty of cheese. Gerard explained that this, along with a fresh baguette, was all a young French bachelor, who travelled a lot for work, required to woo international ladies and generally subsist.

A couple of weeks before I was scheduled to depart France, Gerard came to visit me in Saint-Paul for a few drinks and some reminiscing. He asked what I would do when I returned to Canada to work for my new bosses at Broadcom. I described my new role and added that I wasn't going to work quite so hard anymore. This conjured up a sharp French *la puff* exhale from his lungs, smoke included, and the response, "You can't choose to swim in the fast lane, and yet swim like you are in the slow lane." When I looked at him with puzzled amusement, he continued, "Working at Broadcom is continuing to swim in the fast lane, and if you swim slowly there, you will have all the other intense employees swim over your back and drown you."

And with that he winked, drew on his cigarette and blew a long exhale into the night over his shoulder rather than in my face, because he was an experienced international traveler and knew that we Canadians didn't much care for smoke blown in our faces, and because it added a cool dramatic effect to the words he had just left hanging in the air. I paused, reflected, and said, "*Touché, mon ami*, I'll swim in the fast lane a while longer then, but not forever... France has taught me it's not worth the personal sacrifice."

13

WELCOME TO THE CIRCLE

A S THE flowering Bougainvillea was reaching the peak of its bloom, climbing high on the stones walls of Saint-Paul's ramparts, the village became painted in fuchsia on a gold canvas as the sun set each late-summer evening. I now felt at home here, able to absorb details that had initially escaped me. I knew my way around every narrow cobblestone street, alley, courtyard, and fountain. I was friends, or at least friendly, with many of the shopkeepers, to the point that I didn't feel that I had to stop to talk with them every time I passed. Instead I could say hello by giving a knowing nod or subtle wave without breaking stride as I headed to the pétanque grounds, or to where my car waited in the little dusty parking lot reserved for *riverains* like me.

A clear sign to me that I was now comfortable here was that I could drive the perimeter road that ran inside the walls of my medieval village with the speed and agility that would make recent F1 racing champion Jacques Villeneuve, or his father Gilles before him, proud. My rental Peugeot 407 Coupe, which was a fair stand-in for my previous Renault Mégane, was no Williams Engineering high-horsepower machine, though it was plenty fun to drive on the *autoroutes* and roundabouts of the region, and was nimble enough to navigate the one road inside the Saint-Paul walls with gusto.

That ring road was just wider than my sporty 407. It featured the vertical rock wall of the inside of the ramparts on the right, and on the left either storefronts with tourists stepping out unannounced or the rock walls of the back of shops and apartments draped in lush magenta blankets of Bougainvillea. (Incidentally, I don't really know how to differentiate magenta and fuchsia). Sections of this windy, one-way road resembled early single lane tunnels through the Alps, except that you could see the blue sky of the Côte d'Azur if you dared to look up. The first time I drove this narrow road, I slowed each time it took a sharp bend and crawled forward, being careful not to take off a mirror as I went. But now I drove the road at a near constant speed, knowing exactly when to twitch the wheel slightly left or right to avoid an impact with centuries-old masonry. When my parents visited, I quietly delighted in watching both of them close their eyes and gasp uncontrollably each time I subjected them to my 'Formula One de Saint-Paul' driving.

I never even so much as scratched any of my rental cars, a rare accomplishment based on the appearance of the condition of the rental fleet.

I was also now comfortable with driving *rond-points* [roundabouts] with the gall of a true French driver. As I mentioned earlier, I had learned that the key to roundabout navigation in France is to drive like you are wearing horse blinders, resisting the urge to turn your head to either side. This technique ensures that you do not give in to the oncoming aggressive Frenchman, or woman, seeking to gain advantage by intimidating you, using speed and inertia as weapons. The oncoming driver will only acquiesce to avoid a collision, if you never make even partial eye contact with them. "Gall"—defined in the Merriam-Webster dictionary as "brazen boldness coupled with impudent assurance and insolence"—is definitely the right word to describe the nerve it takes to successfully execute this manoeuvre on a regular basis.

As a Canadian who is relatively well-versed in the separatist history of our fine province of Québec, which I truly love and which is home to my beloved Montréal Canadiens hockey team, I chuckle at using the word "gall" because it reminds me of the time Charles de Gaulle interfered in Canadian politics during a speech he gave on a visit to Québec in 1967. (An aside within an aside: surely the threat of needing to change the name of the iconic Montréal Canadiens hockey team, if Québec ever separates from Canada, should keep our country together, no?)

I was unceremoniously reminded of de Gaulle's famous (or "infamous," depending on one's perspective) speech by an elderly pétanque combatant at a critical moment of a match, one scorching hot and humid afternoon. It was one of the most brilliant examples of mind games that I had been subjected to and, as is often the case, it was both hilarious and clever too. Hubert and I were embroiled in a close match with two older gentlemen, and just as I was about to throw a critical ball in the deciding third game, one of the leathery old guys blurted out with vigour, "*Vive le Québec libre!* [Long live free Quebec!]." De Gaulle had used these words in front of a large outdoor crowd as he concluded a speech from the balcony of Montréal's city hall, placing particular emphasis on the word *libre*, inciting the crowd of sovereignty enthusiasts by implying that France supported their movement and sparking a diplomatic incident with Canada's government.

Unlike that day in Montréal, this time the words were aimed at only one person with the objective to rattle, rather than to inspire. When strung together like that, those four words were naturally irritating to an anglophone, patriotic Canadian, and they forced me to stand up from my ready-to-throw crouch, chuckle, and give him a wink. They had an even greater effect on Hubert, who let out the loudest and most uncontrollable bout of laughter I ever witnessed from anybody on those hallowed pétanque grounds. He laughed so hard he had to take a long walk around the outside of the playing surface to regain his breath and stop guffawing, so that I could recompose myself for my important shot. The good-natured, sarcastic ribbing didn't faze me much and we managed to go on to win that match; with the bonus that I felt a little more part of the old boys' club of Saint-Paul after having been subjected to the jab.

Though he wanted to win that match and we had become as tight as brothers, Hubert couldn't help but be amused by a poke to the ribs of my Englishness from one of his country-men, a fact that he reminded me of several times during the rest of that summer by recounting the "*Vive le Québec libre!*" story in near hysterics whenever he bumped into a friend he hadn't seen in a while. After listening to him tell and retell it, the story started to get old for me. I eventually fired back, while he and his friends were laughing so hard they were nearly choking on their cigarettes. I smirked, let out a French-man-like *la puff* of air, and, to demonstrate that I too could be culturally insulting, said, "*Très drôle mes amis, je suis sûr que de Gaulle aimait ce cadeau bizarre, que les Etats-Unis a envoyés et assemblés pour lui, la tour Eiffel* [Very funny my friends, I'm sure de Gaulle loved that ugly gift that the USA sent over and assembled for him, the Eiffel Tower]," knowing full well that the tower was a cherished French icon that French engineer Gustave Eiffel's company constructed for the 1889 World's Fair, the year before Charles de Gualle was born.

Being drawn into trash talk or even just sharing chuck-les became more and more frequent during matches, and always added warmth to my day. During a match when Hubert and I were not seeing eye to eye on strategy, I made a bit of a mocking gesture while standing beside and a little back of him as he was about to throw. I rolled my eyes and exhaled a Frenchman-like short *la puff* of air, which I thought I had done too subtly to be noticed, but without flinching from his ready-to-*tire* throwing position, he said in English, "Hey, I see you behind my eyes," and then made a nice shot. We chuckled quietly between us for several rounds as we digested his terrible misuse of my language, which was intended to tell me that he could sense my insubordination without even looking at me.

Occasionally the comradery I was developing with local players would extend to include a woman. My favourite female combatant by far was Annette, a middle-aged woman who frequented the pétanque pitch and had a unique calling card that I have never seen since in France; she smoked a pipe that she always had alight in her mouth or hand during matches, whether she was playing or just observing. I felt honoured to be invited to play against Annette a few times, and was always a little bit intimidated by her stoic nature, her long calm drags on that pipe, and the fact that she never played verbal minds games and rarely spoke much at all. This woman was to me the definition of "calm, cool, and collected," emphasis on "cool."

One lazy afternoon after a match concluded, Hubert very matter-of-factly said, "Follow me; Annette has something for you." He then started walking slowly towards the only building that adjoined Saint-Paul's dusty and ancient pétanque grounds other than the café. It was a small humble structure with a sign above the door that read only 'Le Cercle'. What was this? Was Hubert walking me towards the private bar that was off limits to everybody except registered pétanque players of Saint-Paul? Though nobody had ever spoken of it to me, I knew by observation that this building was the exclusive bastion of local long-time players and that I should never try to walk in or ask to be invited.

As we neared the threshold of the entryway, I paused and said to Hubert, "*Vraiment?* [Really?]." He grinned, nodded,

Cercle d'Union Saint-Pauloise
06570 Saint-Paul - Tél: 04 93 32 95 77

Carte de Membre

N° 007

Nom : Shore **Prénom :** Paul

Adresse : 1rue de l'Etoile apt 7

Tél (s) : 0 68645 3148 **Année :** 1999

put his hand on my shoulder, and said nothing but "*Vraiment*." Annette was expecting us; she greeted us at the door and shook my hand and Hubert's. I could hardly believe that I had earned the right to be invited to enter this historical little building that tourists steer well clear of, and that was just the beginning of my amazement. As we took seats at the little bar, Annette asked us what we would like to drink; we both ordered a pastis... of course.

And then came the real surprise! What Annette presented me with next made my eyes well up because, though I had never seen one before, I immediately understood what it was, how rare it was, and that it carried with it a new level of acceptance that I had never expected. She drew an inhale from her pipe and let out a short polite exhale as she handed me a little plastic card the shape and size of a credit card and said, "*Bienvenue à la Cercle* [Welcome to the Circle]." It was my official Saint-Paul pétanque membership card, which would allow me admittance into their private club for life and carried with it a status granted to few. Hubert said I was undoubtedly the first Canadian to be granted one, and that very few foreigners at all had one. I still cherish the card and keep it in a drawer of my den desk, where I can pull it out from time to time to reminisce over.

The number on my card is #607, which confirms Hubert's assertion that there are very few of these little gems in existence. The handwritten number almost looks like "007," which makes me chuckle inside every time I pull it out. I learned to play under the cover of darkness and overcame many battles to emerge as a respected player... Bond, James Bond. My name, local address on *Rue de l'Etoile* (Star Street, I kid you not), telephone number, and the year of issue (1999), also adorn the small white card, as do the most important words printed on it: "Carte de Membre [Member Card]." I thanked Annette and few words were exchanged, though none were really needed because the first-time *bisou* on both my cheeks and her warm smile conveyed the message one more time—Welcome into our circle!

14

IL A LE SENS DU JEU

A FEW TIMES during my year in France, I flew to Paris for the weekend to visit Parisian friends who I had met in Nice and who had moved back to the City of Light only a few months after my arrival. Oddly, the catalyst for my first of these weekends of enlightenment was the opportunity to take part in Friday Night Rollerblading. Paris never ceases to amaze me with its ability to intertwine ancient history and civilization with modern pop culture, in creative ways that keep youth engaged and active. Rollerblading on the Nice boardwalk alongside the Mediterranean Sea seemed completely natural and logical to me, but when my good friend, Sophie, said, "Hey, you should come to Paris for a rollerblading session with thousands of people on a Friday night," I did the type of rapid side-to-side head shake one does when one's ears are full of water or that a Looney Tunes cartoon character does after a concussive blow to the head.

"*Qu'est-ce que tu m'a dit, Sophie?* [What did you say to me, Sophie?]" I asked, to which she responded by explaining that on Friday nights in the summer, after sunset, the city closes a series of streets to cars so that thousands of people can rollerblade together in relative safety for a couple hours. On each of these nights the route passes by a different set of famous city monuments, parks, and gardens. When I asked how Paris could possibly ban all cars from the number of streets that would be traversed over a couple of hours, Sophie explained that they don't have to. Instead of completely closing streets, they provide a police escort at the front and the back of the wheeled throng that typically stretches about two kilometres in length, and lead it like a slithering snake along the predetermined route through the city and its sights.

I was game for new one-of-a-kind experiences and didn't need much of an excuse to head to Paris for a weekend, so off I flew after work on Friday. I connected with Sophie and her friends at her downtown apartment, and we took the métro to Place de la Bastille. When we surfaced from the humid underground, which has a not-so-sweet aroma in the summer that I am sure tourists from around the world have come to know as a uniquely Parisian 'je ne sais quoi', we sat on a curb to lace up our skates. Countless others were doing the same, the magnificently lit July Column monument to the French Revolution of 1830 towering above us. Once the session began and our part of the crowd started to move a few minutes later, we began a skate that would take us past the lit-up Eiffel Tour, Arc de Triomphe, Tuileries Garden, and many more famous and beautiful Paris landmarks. What a memorable, surprising and healthy way to tour Paris and share in the vibe of the youth of the day! I was always grateful that my new French friend had invited me to take part in this piece of present-day Paris culture and allowed me to feel a level of acceptance into modern French life that I rarely got to experience during my year in her country, even if the experience only lasted a couple hours and left my body vibrating all night from wheeling over the uneven, and in places cobblestoned, Paris streets.

It was on another one of these weekend trips to Paris that I first visited the Paris Opera House (*le Palais Garnier*) to attempt to broaden my recent enlightenment by taking in a ballet performance. When we got to our seats and looked up at the ceiling of this majestic building, which is considered a national monument, we were immediately taken aback by the beauty of the large circular mural painted up there. My Saint-Paul immersion enabled me to immediately recognize the work as unmistakably being that of Marc Chagall. Once again, I felt like a cultural boor inside—how was it that only now I was learning about this Chagall masterpiece that most certainly must be world famous?

The ballet was fascinating and the performers amazed me with their athletic ability and stamina, though I would be lying if I said that I became a true fan of the ballet that day or any thereafter. On the way out after the performance, we stopped to read about the history of the mural that I had kept peering up at over and over again during the performance. In 1963, Chagall had been commissioned to paint the new ceiling, after France's minister of culture searched for something unique and decided that the work of Chagall was the ideal fit. His selection caused much controversy. There were those who objected to having a Russian Jew decorate a French national treasure, and others who disliked the choice of any modernist to paint the ceiling of the historic building. Articles condescending to Chagall appeared in some magazines, about which he later commented, "They really had it in for me. It is amazing the way the French resent foreigners. You live here most of your life. You become a naturalized French citizen. Work for nothing decorating their cathedrals, and still they despise you. You are not one of them."

Despite his frustration, the 77-year-old artist continued the project, which took him a year to complete. The wheel-shaped mural, which was roughly 2,400 square feet and required 440 pounds of paint, paid tribute to the composers Mozart, Wagner, Mussorgsky, Berlioz and Ravel, as well as to famous actors and dancers. After it was unveiled, even the most bitter opponents of the commission seemed to fall silent. The press unanimously declared Chagall's new work to be a great contribution to French culture. Several months after seeing the marvelous work, I would begin to relate to this difficulty of being accepted into French culture in a meaningful way, even if my meaningful way was simply to become accepted by my neighbours as a pétanque player. A player who was not only decent at the game, but who also deeply understood and appreciated its nuances and cultural significance.

Another story about Marc Chagall that cemented the connection I was developing for him centered around a letter he published in a Paris weekly a few months after the Allies liberated Paris from Nazi occupation, while he was still living in exile in the U.S. Entitled "To the Paris Artists," it read, "In recent years I have felt unhappy that I couldn't be with you, my friends. My enemy forced me to take the road of exile. On that tragic road, I lost my wife, the companion of my life, the woman who was my inspiration. I want to say to my friends in France that she joins me in this greeting, she who loved France and French art so faithfully. Her last joy was the liberation of Paris... Now, when Paris is liberated, when the art of France is resurrected, the whole world too will, once and for all, be free of the satanic enemies who wanted to annihilate not just the body but also the soul—the soul, without which there is no life, no artistic creativity."[2] A profound passage, though I have always wondered about the choice of words "once and for all," since surely Marc would not have believed that evil would never show its face again in the world, or even just in France. I have come to think that he was either by nature an optimist or was purposely being optimistic to try and help raise the spirit of the French people, and in particular the arts community; either way, I gravitate to this type of positive outlook for the future, no matter how hard times have recently been. And "the soul, without which there is no life" is a powerful phrase—certainly pétanque would have been lost, along with the rest of

2. Chagall, Marc. *Marc Chagall on Art and Culture*, editor: Benjamin Harshav. Stanford Univ. Press (2003)

the soul of France, and the soul of the entire Jewish people and several other minority groups, had the allies not prevailed. Chagall provides yet another strong reminder that we must continue to teach the history of war and genocide and work together globally to ensure that both the body and the soul of all unique cultures from around the world can thrive in peace.

Years after living in Saint-Paul, I asked Hubert why I had never heard a story about Marc Chagall playing pétanque. He wasn't sure, but did some local research and determined with a fairly high level of confidence that Chagall either hadn't played pétanque at all, or at least hadn't played in public view while he lived in Saint-Paul. Was this another example of only ever becoming able to feel 'nearly accepted' within French culture, or was it simply the case of a rather poorly physically coordinated Jewish fella with other strong talents and interests on which to focus? Thinking about it, I decided that if I was Chagall and had arrived in Saint-Paul to live and paint, I probably wouldn't have subjected myself to the torturous process of taking up pétanque either; so maybe the fact that he didn't play the game is nothing more than an example of the day-to-day personal liberty of which France is so proud.

PERSONAL LIBERTY DID not seem to extend to the right to choose to play with or against whomever you wished. I rarely saw anybody play outside their age bracket, which is to say that the roughly ten-year age difference between Hubert and me was about the largest gap I observed between teammates or competing teams. So one day when I was sitting around with my ball-purse in hand watching matches from the sidelines because Hubert was late for our meeting at the pétanque grounds, I was astonished when a group of far older local men asked me if I wanted to join them. They were only three, so I took the gesture of inclusion with a grain of salt—I thought of it more like, "We can't find anybody else around with a pulse, who we know is any good at this game, and we have seen you around here playing better than you look, so would you like to join us?"

My teammate-to-be, Roget, introduced himself with a firm handshake and a soft nod, as did the other two gentlemen in their seventies, who would be our competition. I was oddly relaxed to play with them. It seemed I felt that I had earned this level of respect by playing in the daylight for several months, in view of the doubting eyes of so many leathery-skinned gents like them.

The match wasn't terribly notable and in the end Roget and I lost in three long, close games. I played well, though not magnificently, and the same could be said for my partner. But despite the rather routine nature of the game itself, the day produced possibly my fondest memory from my year in France. Hubert arrived partway through the match and I could see a mix of shock, fear, and pride on his face as he watched his young protégé playing and holding his own with the big boys. It was a pretty special moment when our eyes connected as he saw me playing and gave me a wink, but that wasn't the fondest memory I'm referring to.

There were several matches going on in parallel and a typical assortment of tourists and locals watching from the edges of the grounds. One elderly local onlooker was familiar because I had noticed him playing from time to time, and seen him watching frequently; yes this was the old man of the hilarious "Canada Dry!" barb. I met eyes with him as he stood on the sidelines, arms crossed over his chest and brow furled, surprised to see me playing without Hubert. I would lock eyes with him many more times during this match than usual, probably because Hubert wasn't my teammate and I therefore had much less in-game conversation to occupy my full attention, though possibly because he was trying to size me up now that I was playing without my coach.

I had become a fairly skilled *pointeur*, but an even better strategist. A moment emerged in the match when I didn't play the obvious shot, instead opting to park my ball very close to one of my others that was already in scoring position, so as to protect it from the skilled *tireur* of the other team. I managed to uncork a beautiful shot, my ball gradually rolled its way across the dusty ground with purpose, bouncing over little pebbles and curving towards my other ball until it came to rest directly in line and only millimeters away from it—an outstanding defensive execution, if I do say so myself. As the ball came to a stop, the elderly pétanque connoisseur spoke up quietly but clearly, saying to nobody in particular, yet in a way to everybody within earshot, "*Il a le sens du jeu* [He has a sense for the game]."

I smiled graciously to the old man and nobody else added anything to his remark, though I noticed a few nodding heads. At this point Hubert strolled towards me from the sidelines and while passing by he whispered, "*Tu as entendu ça?* [Did you hear that?]" I gave the slightest of nods and an even slighter smile, without so much as making eye contact with him. With that Hubert continued his stroll past me and back to his viewing position with a bounce in his step like that of a proud father seeing his son bring home his first date to introduce to his parents.

Hubert's behaviour confirmed what I had been thinking; the fact that the old gentleman had said these words out loud was an immense compliment that I should treasure. He didn't say that I was good at the game, but that I really understood it deeply, and with that he was communicating that he knew how difficult it was to reach that level and was congratulating me for having had the chutzpah and determination to get there. So it hardly mattered to me that Roget and I did not go on to win the match. This was the closest I had come yet to experiencing a 'nearly accepted' moment, while in the middle of playing a match, and I was going to bask in the glow of that feeling. Arguably it was the zenith of my acceptance into French culture—"*Il a le sens du jeu*"—wow!

AND EVEN THOUGH it seems that Marc Chagall never played this game, I still imagine today that he would have been delighted at looking in on a Jewish young man with Belarus heritage who had found a way to paint himself a memorable scene within Saint-Paul culture. As would have my kind-hearted grandfather Isaac, who escaped persecution in Lithuania and eventually settled in Canada by way of Sao Paolo, Brazil; and my namesake grandfather Paul, who escaped from Kiev, Prussia, with his parents and also found a new home in Canada.

15

JOIE DE VIVRE

THE SWEET smell of burning vineyard clippings filled the air each morning as autumn crept gently towards winter. In the distance far beyond the rampart walls I could begin to see dustings of snow on the peaks of the Maritime Alps, which reminded me every day that I would be heading back home to Canada soon. I continued to make time for pétanque, especially now because I knew that my time in France was running out. I was determined to squeeze in as many matches as I could, and soak in my new, yet invisible-to-anybody-else status as a member of the Cercle of Saint-Paul.

When the dreaded day finally came to pack up my office in Sophia Antipolis and say goodbye to the administrative staff, I don't know what came over me. As I gave them hugs and *bisous*, I actually started to cry; not just a little misting-up sort of cry, but real waterfall tears down my cheeks. This was an emotion I didn't really know within myself—over years to come, I would see it emerge again, though infrequently, like when I was walked down the aisle by my parents; when my kids were born or reached important life milestones; and when our world lost close friends or family members too young. Once again it rang clear that this place, its people, and its way of life had made a far deeper impact on me than I had ever anticipated.

The very next day, December 30, was to be my last day in France. On my way home to Vancouver, I would cele-brate New Year's with friends in another fascinating place with amusing, heartwarming people; a place where I had also never spent any time before: St. John's, Newfoundland. Nothing like shocking the system back into Canadian life by ringing in the new millennium in one of the most frigid places in the country, by attending an outdoor concert on New Year's Eve put on by the quintessentially Canadian band, Great Big Sea.

But before leaving France, there was one last game of pétanque to play—on my thirty-third birthday no less. I don't even recall our opponents, though I do remember that Hubert and I won easily and were very relaxed throughout, having fun with our last match together for quite some time. The highlight of the event came when I was crouched and ready to throw, and a moped revved its engine just metres away from the grounds. I stayed in my crouch, raised my head and muttered "*Mange merde* [Eat shit]," which sent good old Hubert into one last fit of hysterics. He loved that although I fit in pretty well now, I was still the same old quirky little Canadian, who spoke poor French and knew little about wine, as the guy who had arrived and demanded to be taught to play pétanque a year earlier.

After the match, Hubert and I retired to the café alone for one last pastis together... or was it two or three? When it came time to say goodbye, something happened that had never happened to me in France before. As we reached out to shake hands one last time, Hubert planted a *bisou* on me (both cheeks), which of course I reciprocated without hesitation. Sure, I had been given parting goodbye *bisous* by all my female friends, but the men had only extended a typical warm handshake or perhaps a hug. Not Hubert, though; our relationship was different, more like brothers who were a decade apart in age.

At the start of this story, I defined *bisou* as "The charming manner that the French greet one another with, a ceremonial kiss on both cheeks, which should not to be mistaken for a sign of real affection or even friendship, but rather what I see as a refreshingly warm way of saying hello and goodbye." And I explained that there are exceptions to the rule that a bisou does not convey real affection, one of those being the rare occasion when men exchange the pleasantry.

This *bisou* from Hubert was a clear sign of that "real affection." It was funny, we two "tough guys" trying hard not to show emotion, yet finding it impossible to hide. After the kisses on both cheeks we could hardly look one another in the eyes as we patted each other on the shoulders and turned to walk away, while waving and both exclaiming wishfully "*A bientôt* [See you soon]."

I had learned through becoming intimate with the charming game of pétanque that it is a wonderful metaphor for the game of life: challenges and setbacks to overcome; always new lessons to be learned; risks to take and risks to avoid; relationships to develop and some to let go of. Hubert would be a friend I would have to let go of on a day-to-day basis, though we would likely stay in touch forever—as would I with my new friends, "the south of France" and "the game of pétanque."

I had one more soul to visit before taking the windy back road exit out of the village one last time. He was only a short walk from my apartment, but I purposely took a meandering route so that I could absorb the magical vistas past the rampart walls one last time. I strolled slowly in the chilly December air, as the light began to fade and the shadows lengthened, in no rush to reach my destination. Ripe oranges hung from stout trees along the way, still clinging to their branches after the first winter frost. Leaves and fallen petals swirled in the quiet corners of the village and around the gate to its cemetery. I had visited Marc Chagall's grave several times during my year in Saint-Paul and had decided to pay homage one final time.

It had always struck me that Chagall's crypt with its embossed Star of David was the only such symbol that I could find in the Saint-Paul cemetery. I inferred from this that Chagall had become so attached to this town that he had decided his eternal rest would be more peaceful here than in a Jewish cemetery elsewhere. There were always many pebbles adorning the top of the grave, placed there by visitors who knew this tradition signaling that they had been there to show their respect. I was compelled to pick one up and gently place it atop the crypt alongside the other pebbles, the act nearly bringing me to tears for some odd, powerful, unclear reason. Maybe it was the realization that being laid to rest in Saint-Paul likely signified not only that Marc Chagall was at peace here, but also that he had at long last been accepted by the French people. That realization settled somewhere deep inside me over time; my small breakthrough into French culture through a game played with metal balls didn't hold a candle to the challenges that Marc had overcome as a Jewish artist from Belarus, but it reminded me just how hard it is for any new immigrant to gain true acceptance into the society of an adopting land.

I had read that this gifted man once said, "The dignity of the artist lies in his duty of keeping awake the sense of wonder in the world. In this long vigil he often has to vary his methods of stimulation; but in this long vigil he is also himself striving against a continual tendency to sleep." I have come to appreciate the charming game of pétanque as a fantastic example of a "method of stimulation" that keeps awake one's sense of wonder. Cultural pastimes, like this ancient game, truly serve as energy for aspiring everyday artists, as we work through life's daily challenges. They recharge our *joie de vivre,* our delight in being alive; they free our minds; and they fuel our chutzpah for adventure. We must protect these beautiful little gifts, tie a bow around them, love and keep them safe.

EPILOGUE
DÉJÀ VU

TWO YEARS after my emotional departure, I returned to Saint-Paul de Vence for a vacation and had the audacity to lug my set of heavy pétanque balls along with me. I knew this was risky because if I couldn't play as well as I had when I left, bothering to bring back my personal balls would be an exceedingly bad piece of judgment. Yet I also knew how big of a mind-game advantage it would be to reappear on the pétanque grounds of Saint-Paul with my own equipment in tow, plus it simply made me chuckle that I would even bother to do such a thing. Of course, travelling with three metal objects, that don't look good under airport x-ray scrutiny, adds an odd wrinkle to one's travel experience, but

I was more than happy to sweet talk my way through those minor challenges.

As I entered Saint-Paul the feeling of *déjà vu* in my jet-lagged head nearly overwhelmed me. I don't mean the literal translation of "already seen," because, of course, the village hadn't physically changed much. I mean the phenomenon of experiencing a strong sensation that I had actually travelled back in time. This was brought on by the sense that absolutely nothing had changed; not the very people sitting at Le Café de la Place and what they were drinking and discussing, not the pétanque teams and the mannerisms of each, not even the little rain-worn valleys in the dirt of the pétanque grounds themselves. This deep feeling of familiarity warmed my insides.

Hubert met me with open arms and a *bisou* to both cheeks, though he burst the bubble of my return the moment I proudly showed him that I had brought my own balls with me, by not committing to a time to play our first match of this new era. "You know we aren't sitting around on vacation all the time here," he scoffed with a wry smile that he tried to hide; "I have work to do!" It was a fair comment, though I knew it was made more to make a point and to be funny than because he was really overly busy that day.

Ahhhhhh—I was back in the crusty nation I had so grown to love. If you can survive long enough in France for that crustiness to morph from what appears to be dismissive arrogance—the only form of it most tourists ever get to experience—into the great warmth associated with being part of a tribe that loves sarcasm and the exchange of witty barbs as a normal part of its household manner, you are a lucky person.

I consider myself among those lucky few. That warmth can be buried deep, and it typically takes a long time and a lot of effort to earn it. I had been able to experience that warmth within some circles, though I was realistic enough to understand that my circle didn't extend broadly.

For me there are some clear similarities between the characteristics of the French "tribe" and my ancestral tribe. The witty, and at times deeply cutting, style of banter is an obvious one. As is the "crustiness" that I have seen on display at times within my family, mostly by older relatives from the "old country," who could be rather hard on outsiders. This is probably a well-justified defense mechanism for a people who have felt under attack repeatedly throughout the ages—not dissimilar from the French, who have faced repeated physical and cultural abuses. Even the evolution of English as "the" language for international affairs is an affront to the French that contributes to their desire to fiercely protect their own culture and language. Though once you prove to the tribe that you are genuinely respectful, interested in them, and kind, you can become accepted as an integral part of the inner circle of the family.

Having returned to Hubert's mixed-message welcome, I settled into a front row seat at Le Café de la Place and sipped *un petit café* while eavesdropping to catch up on local affairs. The best gossip was about the new lights hanging above the pétanque grounds from the huge branches of the plane trees. A debate raged about the appropriateness of these new illumination devices. Some viewed them as *"extraordinaire,"* an extraordinary improvement for the pétanque-playing fraternity. Of course, others felt the exact opposite and declared them to be "*trop brilliant* [too bright]" and attention-creat-ing for their subtle game that was supposed to be difficult to play, particularly after dusk.

Hubert eventually came bounding into the café, declar-ing, "We play at once." I was surprised by his pre-game glee, but only until I set eyes on our opponents—it was our old friend Rémy, "The Easily Flappable," and his pal, Jean-François. It was as if Hubert knew exactly how this was going to play out and was already anticipating the joy it would give him. He wasn't wrong; the match turned out to be fantasti-cally entertaining.

Rémy cracked me up the moment he saw me, when he said in French, "Hey, where have you been?" Ah, the south of France, where time stands still—he thought I had only been away for a few weeks. I had to explain that I had been living back in Canada for two years and this was to be my first time playing pétanque since I had departed France. Without hesitation he declared, "*Alors, nous allons vous faire embrasser la Fanny* [Then we will make you kiss the Fanny]." A very bold statement, meaning that he was confident that we were going to be defeated without scoring a single point, a humiliation requiring us to kiss the sculpture behind the bar of the derrière of the legendary barmaid named Fanny. And so the mind games were underway, before the match had even started; par for the course. Hubert laughed out loud in Rémy's face and reminded him that Paul, '*le petit Canadien,*' had in fact never had to kiss the Fanny, and this wasn't going to be the day that changed.

For good measure, Hubert then added in English, "He kicked your ass two years ago, and he will kick your ass again today." It seems Rémy did understand some English after all because the look on his face turned stern the moment he absorbed those words. Just like in the past, Rémy had taken the first stab at mental jousting, only to have Hubert set him back on the heels of his grey matter with a verbal blow to his amygdala. And for good measure, Hubert added, "*Et regardez, il a apporté ses propres boules* [and look, he brought his own balls]," just to amplify the unsettling ringing that was now occurring between Rémy's ears.

The match began slowly and I have to admit that I was rusty for the first game, with Hubert having to carry us to a narrow win by making some great shots. The second game of the match was just like old times though. I found my zone and began playing like I had never been away. Not surprisingly, Rémy's game melted down faster than warm Brie on a fresh baguette left out in the sun on a summer afternoon in Provence.

This time Rémy's mental implosion was something special, even for him. It started fairly traditionally with repeated mutterings of "*Ce n'est pas possible* [It's not possible]" each time I made a great shot. After one particularly crazy-good shot of mine he came uncorked and began to rant, "*C'est impossible qu'un Canadien* [it's not possible that a Canadian], *qui ne vit pas ici* [who doesn't live here], *peut revenir hier* [can return just yesterday], *et jouer aussi bien* [and play this well]; *c'est impossible* [it's not possible]." I reached out to put my hand on his shoulder to try to calm him down, but he stepped back away from me before I could touch him and yelled, "*Ne me touchez pas* [don't touch me]; *vous êtres le diable* [you are the devil]."

Some things never change indeed; or if they do they only become more intense, not less. When it was clear that the match was going to end in victory for Hubert and me, Rémy asked, "*Combien de temps restez-vous dans la ville?* [How long are you staying in town?]," and when I answered "*Seulment deux jours* [Only two days]," he made a long, slow, relaxed exhale and said calmly, "*Très bien; puis-je vous conduire à l'aéroport?* [Very good; can I drive you to the airport?]," as he winked and grinned. The match ended two games to nil, and Rémy and Jean-François narrowly avoided a trip to kiss the Fanny after being trounced in the second game—I was actually glad that didn't happen to my friend Rémy, despite how much I enjoyed winding him up and how much Hubert would have liked to have seen such a kiss.

Observing this kind of passion for an ancient game that is mostly played socially, confirms for me that pétanque is one of the surviving morsels of French culture that will be protected for a very long time.

Experiencing time standing still can be a comforting feeling—*déjà vu.*

A CLOSING NOTE

WE HAVE used a very special photo of Marc Chagall seated in front of one of his works at the start of the chapter "Becoming a Riverain." The photo was taken by famed photographer Yousuf Karsh in 1965, one year before I was born. It is a striking image of Chagall's joyous spirit, but my fondness for it runs much deeper.

Yousef Karsh fled the Armenian genocide in Turkey in 1924 and eventually settled in Ottawa, in a similar manner to which two of my grandparents and many of my great-aunts and great-uncles fled genocide in Lithuania, Latvia and Belarus around the same period and settled in Ottawa, Montreal and Toronto. In 1937, Karsh was somehow hired to photograph my grandmother, Eve Shore, almost exactly one year before she gave birth to her first child, my father Stephen. The result was a striking portrait of her in the prime of her youth on an art deco set. It graces my home office today. Only a few years later Karsh would gain fame for his stunning photos of royalty, heads of state and celebrities.

All this makes Karsh's photo of Chagall, with one of his paintings (including a view of Saint-Paul de Vence) behind him, extremely meaningful to me. An immigrant Canadian who photographed my grandmother before he gained world acclaim would 28 years later photograph immigrant Marc Chagall in front of a painting of Saint-Paul de Vence, where this grandchild of immigrant Canadians—me—would accidentally come to live another 34 years afterwards. Every time I look at this photo of Chagall, I can't help but smile and take a deep breath, as I spend a moment reflecting on the importance of chance, both in the sense of chance occurrences and, more importantly, being afforded new chances in life.

ABOUT THE AUTHOR

P AUL SHORE is a technology industry veteran who has worked around the globe. His drive to embrace new challenges has seen Paul involved in a variety of pursuits. After the software startup he was with in France was acquired by computer chip maker Broadcom in 1999, Paul returned to Vancouver and led the company's voice-over-internet group for years. Marrying a talent for business with a passion for sport and community, Shore pursued a role in the world of sports and spent an inspiring, and at times physically risky, few years working for the 2010 Olympic and Paralympic Games. He has also regularly dedicated energy to volunteerism, while living in Whistler with his wife and children and exploring the mountains and ocean of the coast.

CPSIA information can be obtained
at www.ICGtesting.com
Printed in the USA
LVOW10s1849010817
543422LV00003B/570/P